SCIENCE FACTS

Glen Vecchione

Illustrated by Joel & Sharon Harris

STERLING

New York / London

www.sterlingpublishing.com/kids

For Sheila Barry-- editor and friend. You will be missed.

Library of Congress Cataloging-in-Publication Data Available

LOT#: 10 9 8 7
08/14

Published by Sterling Publishing Co., Inc.
387 Park Avenue South, New York, NY 10016
© 2004 by Glen Vecchione

Distributed in Canada by Sterling Publishing
c/o Canadian Manda Group, 165 Dufferin Street
Toronto, Ontario, Canada M6K 3H6
Distributed in the United Kingdom by GMC Distribution Services,
Castle Place, 166 High Street, Lewes, East Sussex, England BN7 1XU
Distributed in Australia by Capricorn Link (Australia) Pty. Ltd.
P.O. Box 704, Windsor, NSW 2756, Australia

Printed in China
All rights reserved

Sterling ISBN-13: 978-1-4027-4981-0
        ISBN-10: 1-4027-4981-3

For information about custom editions, special sales, premium and
corporate purchases, please contact Sterling Special Sales
Department at 800-805-5489 or specialsales@sterlingpub.com.

CONTENTS

Introduction

In this book you'll find more than 1,000 interesting and unusual science facts about animals, space, medicine, weather, and the earth—and that's just a start. We've also collected some choice tidbits about inventions, chemistry, plants, computers, and maybe the most interesting scientific subject of all—people. So why do people love facts? Probably because facts are like little stories. They can tell us something new about a subject we thought we already knew all about. Or they can tell us something new, period. Having lots of unusual facts in your head makes you seem smart and interesting.

And using a well-chosen fact to start a conversation is a great way to make a new friend or amuse an old one.

Try out some of these the next time you're eating lunch with the usual crowd and the talk gets a little dull:

- Catfish have over 30,000 taste buds. Humans have about 9,000.

- Parrots can't eat chocolate.

- There are about 32 million bacteria on every square inch of the human body.

We think your friends will beg for more. You can be sure that *The Little Giant Book® of Science Facts* will keep you well supplied with fascinating and entertaining science facts for years to come.

So delight yourself and delight your friends. Facts are just plain fun—and that's a fact!

We have much to learn from the birds and bees—not to mention the goldfish, ostrich, hummingbird, and lowly termite. Have fun discovering some unfamiliar facts about familiar creatures.

1

The blue whale is the world's largest mammal, weighing about 50 tons at birth and 150 tons full-grown. The largest one ever seen alive was a 113.5 foot (34m), 170-ton female.

The world's smallest mammal is the bumblebee bat of Thailand, weighing less than a penny.

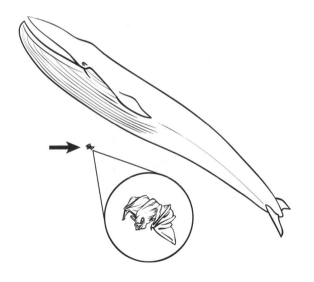

The whistle of the blue whale is the loudest sound produced by any animal—188 decibels!

Gray whales migrate farther than any other animal—about 12,000 miles (19,312km) each year.

LIVING TORPEDOS

Orcas, or killer whales, destroy sharks by swimming very fast and using their snouts to torpedo the shark's soft underside. The impact causes the shark to explode.

Sharks have one of the best immune systems in the animal kingdom. Studies show that they resist every disease, including cancer.

All clams start out as males, but some change into females later in their lives.

A goldfish turns white or light yellow if you keep it in the dark or place it in a body of running water, such as a stream. The more familiar orange pigment develops to protect a fish that's not moving from the sun's ultraviolet radiation.

The Pacific Giant Octopus is the largest octopus in the world. In its two-year lifespan, it grows from the size of a pea to a 30-foot (9m) wide, 150-pound (68kg) monster.

An octopus's mouth is a bony beak located directly under its fleshy head.

The giant squid is the largest creature without a backbone. It can weigh up to 3 tons and grow to nearly 60 feet (18m) long.

Porpoises can be taught to recognize reflections of themselves. Some will even preen and pose before a mirror!

A male saltwater catfish keeps the eggs of his young in his mouth until they are ready to hatch. During this three-week incubation period, he will not eat.

Freshwater catfish have over 30,000 taste buds. Humans have about 9,000.

A female mackerel can lay about 500,000 eggs at one time.

It takes a lobster about seven years to grow to weigh one pound.

Mammals have red blood, insects have yellow blood, and the blood of lobsters is clear—but it turns blue when exposed to oxygen.

It's hard—even for fingerprint experts—to distinguish koala bear fingerprints from human ones.

Chimpanzees spend about a quarter of their lives walking on two legs instead of four.

A cow produces the equivalent of nearly 200,000 glasses of milk in her lifetime.

The American opossum has the shortest gestation period in the animal kingdom—about 12 days after conception. The Asiatic elephant has the longest—608 days, or just over 20 months.

When an opossum plays "possum," it has actually passed out in terror.

A camel's milk never curdles.

To protect themselves from blowing sand, camels have a third eyelid called a *nictitating membrane*.

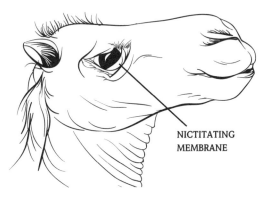

NICTITATING
MEMBRANE

An 1872 virus epidemic destroyed nearly a quarter of America's horse population.

SLEEPWALKING HORSES

Firehouses traditionally have circular stairways because the early fire engines, kept on the ground floor, were pulled by horses. When the horses were stabled, they would often break out and walk up the straight staircases—surprising many a sleeping fireman!

A mule is the offspring of a female horse and a male donkey. The offspring of a male horse and a female donkey is called a hinny.

No new animal has been domesticated in the last 4,000 years.

A newborn kangaroo is about 1 inch (2.5cm) in length.

GREEN EGGS AND HAM?

Feeding hens certain dyes causes the yolks of their eggs to take on the color.

Most light-skinned animals—including pigs, walruses, and light-colored horses—can get sunburned.

Elephants can communicate using sounds between 14 and 35 hertz—well below the range of human hearing.

All polar bears are left-handed.

Carnivorous animals will avoid eating another animal if it has been hit by lightning.

When bats fly out of a cave, they always turn left.

Of all the land animals, howler monkeys are the loudest. Their calls can be heard over two miles away.

The turkey was named for what was wrongly thought to be its country of origin.

One of the longest hibernation periods in the animal kingdom is that of the snail. A snail can sleep for nearly three years without eating.

The mucus trail that a snail produces is so effective that a snail can travel across the edge of a razor without getting cut.

The fastest speed recorded for a garden snail was 0.0313 miles (0.05km) per hour.

Earthworms are made up of many segments called annuli. These annuli are covered in tiny hairs that grip the soil, allowing the worm to move as it contracts its muscles.

A chameleon's body is only half the length of its tongue.

The capybara is an Amazon water hog that looks like a guinea pig, except that it weighs more than 100 pounds (45kg)! It is the world's largest rodent.

A healthy mole can tunnel through 300 feet (90m) of earth in one day.

One female wild golden hamster, found with a litter of 12 in Syria in 1930, is the ancestor of all pet hamsters found today.

THE HIGH COST OF FUR

The average high-quality mink coat requires 35–65 pelts. Beaver coats require 15 pelts; fox, 25; ermine, 150; and up to 120 pelts for the fanciest coat of all—the chinchilla.

Beaver teeth are so sharp and hard that Native Americans used them as knife blades and arrowheads.

Rats are considered one of the most truly omnivorous creatures. They'll eat anything—including dead and dying members of their own species.

Native to Asia, rats spread throughout the world because they often found their way onto ships.

A rat can survive longer without water than a camel.

A single poison-arrow frog, found in the Amazon rainforest, has enough nerve toxin to kill about 2,500 people.

Certain species of frogs can survive subzero temperatures, even if they're completely encased in a block of ice.

Owls have tubular-shaped eyeballs, which makes it impossible for them to move their eyes in their sockets.

The hollow bones of an owl weigh less than its feathers. Hollow bones are found in many bird species—including the pigeon—and help the birds fly with less effort.

Mockingbirds imitate any sound—from a squeaking door to a meowing cat. In urban areas, they can even mimic car alarms and cell phone rings!

Cranes fly as high as 5,000 feet (1,500m) during migration. But in Asia, migrating cranes on their way to India must cross the Himalayan mountains and reach heights of 20,000 feet (6,000m)—four miles up!

The fastest speed ever recorded for a flying bird was 220 miles (352km) per hour. The bird was the spine-tailed swift. The swift is such a speedy flyer that it has lost the ability to walk!

Hummingbirds are nature's smallest birds. They're so tiny that one of their enemies is an insect—the praying mantis.

Hummingbirds, loons, kingfishers, grebes, and swifts are all birds that cannot walk.

The hummingbird is the only bird that can fly backwards.

The brain of a mature ostrich is about the size of a golf ball, slightly smaller than its eye.

An ostrich sticks its head in the sand to search for water.

In ancient Rome, ostriches were bred for strength, and sometimes were even used to pull chariots.

Ostrich eggs are nature's largest eggs and can reach a length of 9 inches (23cm), though they are usually from 6 to 8 inches (15 to 20cm) long. Because of their size and the thickness of their shells, they take up to 40 minutes to hard-boil.

The flightless kiwi bird of New Zealand lives in a hole in the ground, is almost blind, and lays only one egg each year. Despite this, the kiwi has survived for more than 70 million years.

A chemical in chocolate, theobromide, is poisonous to many species of bird, including the parrot. The skins and pits of avocados are also dangerous.

Most parrots have a vocabulary of about 20 words.

Flamingoes can swallow only with their heads upside down.

Baby robins eat an average of 14 feet (4.2m) of earthworms every day.

It's a myth that throwing instant rice at weddings creates a danger for birds. Birds have no problem digesting expanding seeds since these occur regularly in bird diets.

The praying mantis is the only insect that can turn its head from side to side.

There are more insects in one square mile of rural land than there are people on the entire earth.

Aphids are born pregnant without ever having mated. Only 10 days after being born, aphid babies can give birth themselves.

There are more than 900,000 known species of insect in the world, and several new species are discovered each year.

Insect pests eat one third of the world's food crop each year.

Mosquitoes cause more human deaths in the world than any other insect or animal. The diseases they carry include malaria, encephalitis, yellow fever, and West Nile virus.

Mosquitoes avoid citronella because it irritates their feet.

Mosquitoes prefer children to adults, and blondes to brunettes. Skin thickness is probably a factor in this choice.

A cricket must be full-grown before it can chirp. Only then are its wings large and thick enough to produce a chirping sound when rubbed together.

Two of the spiders that are most poisonous to humans are the black widow and the brown recluse. You can recognize the black widow by the red hourglass marking on its side. The brown recluse spider is somewhat smaller (its body and legs cover the size of a large coin), and it has a fiddle or violin marking on its back.

The poison of a female black widow spider is more potent than that of a rattlesnake.

The daddy longlegs spider releases a foul-smelling chemical from the front of its body as a defense against predators. This chemical can cause serious allergic reactions in susceptible individuals.

The common honeybee kills more people than all poisonous snakes combined.

Although there are three general types of spider web, every web is unique.

The average worker bee will produce only one twelfth of a teaspoon of honey in its entire lifetime.

Only one of a queen bee's eggs will survive to become the new queen. The first bee to hatch and emerge from its cell will break open the cells of the competing bees and bite them to death.

The dragonfly can fly 50 to 60 miles (80 to 96km) per hour and is one of the fastest flying insects in the world.

MIXED MESSAGES

When you disturb an ant, it secretes a chemical signal called a pheromone that rapidly diffuses through the air. Within a certain radius of the ant, the pheromone conveys the message "Flee!" to other ants. Outside that radius, the message changes to "Close in and attack!"

An ordinary black ant can lift 50 times its own weight and pull 30 times its own weight.

An ant always falls over on its right side when poisoned with an insecticide.

Ants never sleep.

Worker ants may live seven years, and the queen ant may live as long as 15 years.

Termites found in Australia can build mounds 20 feet (6m) high and at least 100 feet (30m) wide.

Even with its head cut off, a cockroach can live several weeks before it starves to death.

Certain cockroaches prefer the warmth of your inner ear and will crawl in while you sleep.

The scales of the poisonous copperhead snake smell like fresh-cut cucumbers.

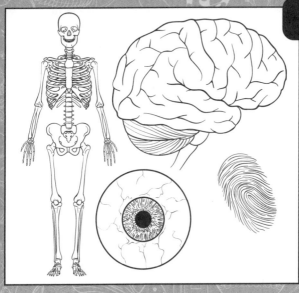

2

A human being is a strange conglomeration of muscles, tissues, organs, and fluids. We also have inexplicable emotions and perplexing behaviors. For thousands of years, we humans have been trying to figure ourselves out—but the puzzle continues.

There are more than 50 trillion cells in the adult human body.

It takes 10 years for the cell structure of the skeleton to completely rejuvenate itself.

Ninety-nine percent of the calcium your body stores is found in your bones and teeth.

Enamel, found in your teeth, is the hardest material in your body.

Electrical nerve impulses travel at more than 250 miles (400 km) per hour throughout the brain and spinal cord.

The human head contains 22 bones.

The human neck has the same number of vertebrae as a giraffe's.

The longest, strongest bone in the body is the femur, or thigh bone.

The lungs of an average adult, unfolded and flattened out, would cover an area the size of a tennis court.

The left lung is smaller than the right lung to make room for the heart.

When fully inflated, an adult's lungs can hold about 3 liters (0.79 gallons) of air.

The largest human organ is the skin, with a surface area of about 25 square feet (2.25 square meters).

Humans shed about 600,000 particles of skin every hour, about 1.5 pounds (0.675kg) a year. By 70 years of age, the average person will have lost 105 pounds (48kg) of skin.

The *stratum corneum* is the thick, tough layer of skin that covers the fingers and the soles of the feet.

There are 45 miles (72km) of nerves in the skin of a human being.

The longest type of cell in the human body is a nerve cell.

There are about 100 billion nerve cells, or neurons, in the human brain.

The term *plexus* refers to the network of blood vessels or nerves that interweave together, such as those on the surface of your skin.

The *gluteus maximus* or buttock muscle is the largest muscle in your body.

If the small intestine were stretched out, it would reach a length of 20 feet (6m).

The longest single nerve in the human body is called the *sciatic nerve*. It runs through the leg and into the buttocks.

The shoulder is the only joint in the human body that can rotate 360 degrees.

The knee is the largest joint in the human body.

Babies are born without kneecaps. They don't appear fully formed until the child reaches nearly six years of age.

Because an infant's brain grows so quickly, the plates of its skull do not fuse together for several years.

Fingerprints appear in a fetus by the age of three months.

Fingerprints evolved to provide better traction for picking up things.

Every second, five people are born and two people die. This results in a net gain of three new people per second.

The cornea, or clear lens of the eye, is the only part of the human body that has no blood supply. It takes oxygen directly from the air.

The hard little lump of flesh in front of your ear canal is called a tragus.

Every minute, 300 million cells die in the human body.

The human brain is about 85 percent water.

The brain consumes about one-fifth of all the calories we take in. It burns more energy than any other organ of the body. Therefore, the "brain power" used in mathematical or linguistic problem-solving can be as effective for losing weight as aerobic exercise.

The left side of the brain controls logic and speech; the right side controls creative thinking and imagery.

A single brain cell can communicate with as many as 25,000 other cells at one time.

A modern human's brain is smaller than a Neanderthal's was.

Waking up to a beeping alarm clock traumatizes the nervous system and can lead to heart attacks in susceptible people. Soft music on a clock radio is the safer alternative.

The air released from a sneeze can exceed a speed of 100 mph (160km/h). The air released from an explosive cough can move at 60 mph (96km/h).

When you sneeze, all bodily functions stop—even your heart.

The human heart beats about 70 times per minute. At this average rate, your heart will have beaten over two and a half billion times by the age of 70.

Your heart pumps 3,600 gallons (13,623L) of blood in one day.

The aorta is the largest artery in the human body.

Your body makes 10 billion white blood cells every day.

Another word for white blood cell is *macrophage*. It means "big eater," referring to the fact that white cells absorb harmful bacteria.

In a human, the only cells without a nucleus are the red blood cells.

There are about five million red blood cells in a tiny droplet of blood.

It takes about 20 seconds for a red blood cell to circulate through the whole body.

A red blood cell has a lifespan of about 120 days.

Every square inch of human skin contains about 20 feet (6m) of blood vessels.

Average humans have 93,000 miles of blood vessels in their body.

It takes about six months for a toenail, and three months for a fingernail, to grow from the base to the tip.

TO GROW OR NOT TO GROW

After about 18 years of age, the human eye remains the same size, with the exception of the lens. The lens of the eye continues to grow throughout life so that it eventually becomes thicker and less transparent. The reduced transparency filters out short wavelength colors like blues and purples, so that we see less of these colors as we grow older. What other parts of the face grow throughout your life? Your nose and ears.

The pop you get when you crack your knuckles is a bubble of gas escaping from the joints between finger bones.

A pack-a-day smoker will lose approximately two teeth every ten years.

Beards are the fastest growing hairs on the human body. If the average man never trimmed his beard, it would grow nearly 30 feet (9m) long in his lifetime.

Humans have as much facial and body hair as the other hairy primates, but it's short, fine, and not easily seen.

The hairs on your arms are programmed to stop growing every couple of months, so they stay short. But the hair follicles on your head are programmed to grow for years at a time, so this type of hair can grow very long.

An average human scalp has 100,000 hairs.

Every human being has a unique smell shared by no other human being.

Humans are the only primates that don't have dark pigment in the palms of their hands.

Midgets and dwarfs almost always have normal-sized children, even if their partners are midgets or dwarfs.

THE EYE'S FAVORITE COLORS

Much of the sun's visible radiation is in the yellow and green range—colors the human eye is most sensitive to. Many communities are taking advantage of this natural preference for yellow light by coloring their emergency vehicles yellow instead of the traditional red.

When you're born you have 300 bones, but by adulthood you have only 206. The 94 bones that "disappear" actually fuse with other bones, such as the separate pieces of skullcap that combine to become the skull.

If locked in an airtight room, you will die by breathing your own carbon dioxide, which is poisonous, rather than from lack of oxygen.

The hyoid is the only bone in the human body not connected to another bone. It's V-shaped and located at the base of the tongue between the mandible and the voice box. It supports the tongue and its muscles.

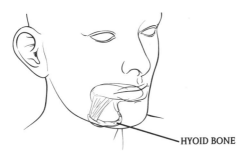

HYOID BONE

If you yelled for eight years, seven months, and six days, you would produce enough sound energy to heat an eight-ounce cup of coffee.

The vocabulary of the average person consists of 5,000 to 6,000 words.

PHARAOH FUEL

Because mummies were so plentiful in late 19th century Egypt, they were used as fuel for locomotives. Mummies burned well and were considered much less valuable than scarce wood and coal supplies. Mummies were also shipped to England to be used as both fuel and fertilizer.

During sleep, one man in eight snores, and one in ten grinds his teeth.

There are on average 32 million bacteria on every square inch of the human body.

Of all human fears, the fear of public speaking is at the top of the list. The fear of heights is next, and the fear of spiders takes third place. The fear of dying comes in a remote 23rd on the list.

Humans can detect between 2,000 and 4,000 odors. This number decreases as we age.

Most people lose half their taste buds by 60 years of age.

Women burn about 50 fewer calories of fat than men do each day.

The jaw muscles of a human being provide up to 200 pounds (90kg) of psi, or pressure per square inch, during the chewing process.

Lab tests can detect traces of alcohol in urine six to twelve hours after a person has stopped drinking.

Your feet contain one quarter of all the bones in your body.

While camels can lose up to 30 percent of their body water in perspiration and continue to cross the desert, humans would die of dehydration after losing only 12 percent of their body water.

In five years, a woman who wears lipstick will use enough to draw a line equal to her height.

HUMAN HARDWARE STORE

The average human body contains:
* Enough iron to make a three-inch nail
* Enough sulfur to kill all the fleas on an average dog
* Enough carbon to make 900 pencils
* Enough potassium to fire a toy cannon
* Enough fat to make seven bars of soap
* Enough phosphorus to make 2,200 match heads
* Enough water to fill a ten-gallon (38L) tank.

Succedaneous teeth refer to the permanent teeth that erupt to replace primary or baby teeth.

The disease varicella was nicknamed "chicken pox" in the 19th century because the lesions resembled chickpeas.

It takes 17 muscles to smile and 43 muscles to frown.

Sleep deprivation is more physically damaging than food deprivation. A person deprived of sleep for ten days can show permanent memory damage and have recurring psychotic episodes.

A person deprived of food for several weeks will be weak but can be returned to health.

The human stomach produces a new layer of mucus every two weeks. Without the new layer, it would digest itself.

Six-year-olds laugh an average of 300 times a day.

Adults laugh only 15 to 100 times a day. Laughing lowers levels of stress hormones and strengthens the immune system.

The female ovum or egg cell is the largest cell in the human body. It is about 1/180 inch (0.138mm) in diameter. The smallest cell is the male sperm. It takes about 175,000 sperm cells to weigh as much as a single egg cell.

You can't kill yourself by holding your breath.

The strongest muscle in the body is the tongue, and every tongue has a unique print.

THE TOUGHEST TONGUE TWISTER

Because of the complex brain and motor coordination it requires, this tongue twister is probably the most difficult in the English language:

"Sixth sick sheik's sixth sheep's sick."

The average human produces 25,000 quarts (23,650L) of saliva in a lifetime, enough to fill two swimming pools.

If you go blind in one eye, you'll lose only about one-fifth of your vision, but all of your depth perception.

The average bank teller loses about $250 every year.

Orange juice helps the body absorb iron more easily.

The average person uses the bathroom six times each day.

THE LONGEST WORD

The longest word in the English language is pneumonoultramiscroscopicsilicovolcanoconiosis, an inflammatory lung disease caused by the inhalation of fine silica or quartz dust.

Women's hearts beat faster than men's.

Offered a new pen to write with, 97 percent of all people will write their own name.

Women shoplift four times more often than men.

If Barbie were life-size, her measurements would be 39-23-33. She would stand seven feet, two inches (218cm) tall, and have a neck twice the length of a normal human neck.

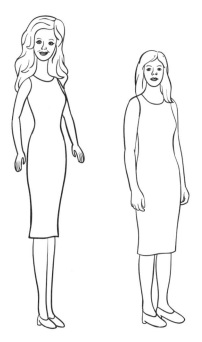

Every human being spends about half an hour as a single cell.

The ashes of the average cremated person weigh nine pounds.

You blink over 10,000,000 times a year.

Over 60 percent of professional boxers have suffered brain damage.

The ancient Romans had a room for bulimic members of the imperial family. Called the vomitarium, it allowed dinner guests to vomit before returning to the table for the next course.

The average person falls asleep in seven minutes.

Men commit suicide three times more frequently than women do. But women attempt suicide two to three times more often than men.

BAD VIBES AT WORK

A United States Department of Justice study conducted between 1992 and 1996 found that 1.7 million Americans experience workplace violence each year. The occupations that were most affected were police officers (306,000), security guards (218,000), taxi drivers (184,000), prison guards (117,000), bartenders (91,000), mental health professionals (80,000), and gas station attendants (79,000).

Left-handed people make up about 10 percent of the world's population.

The average person is about a quarter of an inch (0.6cm) taller at night.

The heart is about the same size as your fist.

Blondes have more hair than dark-haired people.

A Saudi Arabian woman can get a divorce if her husband doesn't give her coffee.

There were 22 Hitlers listed in the New York City phone book in 1940. By 1945, there were none.

The average person walks the equivalent of twice around the world in a lifetime—about 50,000 miles (80,450km).

The most common blood type in the world is Type O positive. The most rare, AB negative, is found in less than 1 percent of the population worldwide.

CROSS-LEGGED MUSCLE

The *sartorius* is the longest muscle in the human body. This narrow muscle passes obliquely across the front of the thigh and helps rotate the leg to the position assumed when sitting cross-legged. Its name comes from the word "sartorial," the traditional cross-legged position of tailors (or "sartors") at work.

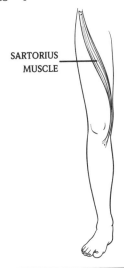

SARTORIUS MUSCLE

The human body has over 600 muscles that comprise 40 percent of the body's weight.

A hiccup is caused by an involuntary spasm in the large flat muscle called the *diaphragm*. The diaphragm muscle separates the chest and the abdominal cavities and helps your chest widen when you breathe in and contract when you breathe out. This is why a spasm in the diaphragm can be such a violent physical sensation.

Every day, the average person releases nearly a pint of intestinal gas. Most is due to swallowed air. The rest is from fermentation of undigested food.

According to German researchers, the risk of a heart attack is higher on Monday than any other day of the week.

The thumb has a separate region reserved for it in the brain.

More people are killed annually by donkeys than die in air crashes.

Your body temperature rises slightly as you digest a large meal.

The sound of a snore can reach up to 69 decibels— almost as loud as the noise of a pneumatic drill.

Every time you lick a stamp, you're consuming one tenth of a calorie.

An average human drinks about 16,000 gallons of water (60,500L) in a lifetime.

Washing your hands is the single most important thing you can do to prevent the transmission of infectious organisms.

The most common name in the world is Mohammed.

A person afflicted with hexadectylism has six fingers or six toes on one or both hands and feet.

3

Familiar things can behave in strange ways. Some of the most everyday foods—celery, apples, ketchup—contain surprises you wouldn't imagine. And some of the more exotic substances, like strontium and "butter of arsenic," may affect your life in more ways than you know. Read on.

If a cup of ketchup left the bottle and traveled indefinitely in a vacuum, it would move at the rate of 25 miles (40km) per year.

Ketchup was sold in the 1830s as a medicine to "fortify the blood."

A nondairy creamer is flammable because it contains so much palm oil.

A powerful glass cleaner, used in the semiconductor industry, is made from a mixture of sulfuric acid and hydrogen peroxide. The mixture is so corrosive when applied to organic materials that it has been nicknamed the "piranha solution."

Murphy's Oil Soap is the chemical most commonly used to clean elephants.

Correction fluid was invented in 1951 by Bette Nesmith Graham. She is the mother of former Monkee Mike Nesmith.

The unique burn of a sparkler is caused by the tiny explosions of minute iron particles ejected from the rod. Iron, separated into fine enough particles, is very combustible.

Celery has "negative calories," which means that it takes more calories to eat a piece of celery than the celery contains as a food.

The molecule for the flavor of spearmint, when reversed, becomes the molecule for the flavor of rye.

Most lipstick, nail polish, artists' paints, and ceramics contain a silvery substance called "pearl essence," obtained from the scales of herring and other fishes.

A chipped pearl will melt in vinegar. This is because under the pearly coating, or nacre, a pearl is mostly calcium carbonite, which dissolves in the acidic vinegar.

Every diamond has its own unique crystal "fingerprint."

Diamonds are crystals formed almost entirely of carbon, such as the charred material left over when you burn a piece of wood.

If you heat a diamond to 1,400 degrees Fahrenheit (760 degrees Celsius), it will simply vanish and leave nothing—not even ash—behind.

Amber, a semiprecious mineral formed by the fossilization of pine resin, was thought in ancient times to be solidified sunshine.

In 19th century America, gallstones from animals were often used to treat infected wounds. A stone was soaked in warm water to soften it so that it could then be applied to the wound. The chemicals in the tissue of the gallstone were believed to neutralize the infection.

The plastic leather called Naugahyde was created and named in Naugatuck, Connecticut.

The top layer of a wedding cake, called the "Groom's Cake," is usually a preserved fruitcake made to last until the couple's first anniversary.

The glue on Israeli postage stamps is certified kosher.

Glass is made by combining sand, soda ash, limestone, and other materials. Nearly 80 percent of the stuff used for making glass bottles and jars comes from recycled bottles and jars!

Recycling one glass jar saves enough energy to power a television for three hours. This is because making new glass from raw materials uses resources—water, sand, mining materials—and produces pollution.

Drinking water after eating reduces the acid in your mouth by 61 percent. It also reduces the acid in your stomach and can lead to indigestion.

The 400 milligrams of nicotine that average pack-a-day smokers inhale in a week would instantly kill them if ingested in a single hour.

Nutmeg is extremely poisonous if injected intravenously.

Some toothpastes contain antifreeze, which acts as an emulsifier to keep the ingredients of the toothpaste from separating at cold temperatures.

FROZEN EXPANSE

Ice is the only substance that expands when frozen instead of contracting. This is because lower temperatures change the tight tetrahedral arrangement of hydrogen and oxygen molecules into wide crystalline rings that take up much more space. This is also why ice, being less dense than liquid water, floats.

When exposed to electricity, the mineral quartz vibrates at regular intervals. The quartz crystal in your wristwatch vibrates 32,768 times a second.

If you apply pressure to a piece of quartz, it generates weak electrical voltage. The voltage is proportional to the degree of pressure applied. This quality in quartz is called piezoelectric—from the Greek word *piezo*, meaning pressure.

Pure gold is so soft and pliable that it can be molded with the hands. A lump the size of a matchbox can be flattened into a foil sheet the size of a tennis court. And an ounce of gold can be stretched into a wire 50 miles (80km) long.

Mercury is the only metal that is liquid at room temperature.

Worcestershire sauce is basically a thin paste made from anchovies and tomatoes—a kind of anchovy "ketchup."

The lava lamp was developed by a man named Craven Walker after he noticed the interesting behavior of melted wax suspended in water.

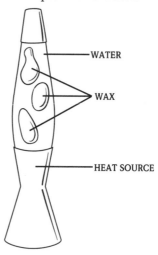

WATER

WAX

HEAT SOURCE

Because of its water-retention properties, plaster of Paris is a natural fire retardant. But at about 600 degrees Fahrenheit (316 degrees Celsius), the stored water is released. This is why walls are often "sweaty" after a fire.

Arrowroot, an antidote for poisoned arrows, is used as a thickener in cooking.

In most television commercials advertising milk, a mixture of white paint and a little turpentine thinner is used to simulate real milk. To the camera, the paint and turpentine mixture looks thicker and richer than real milk. Truth-in-advertising conventions discourage using what would seem like the more natural choice—cream—for a milk ad.

Natural gas has no odor. The smell comes from adding another inert gas called methyl mercaptan to natural gas. This odorant allows leaks to be detected.

In 17th century London, coffee advertisements claimed that the beverage was a cure for scurvy, melancholy, gout, and alcoholism.

A shipload of tainted cocoa, delivered from the American colonies in 1689, was cited as the reason several dozen prominent Londoners died or became violently ill.

In chemistry experiments, a "Pauling Point" refers to the point at which the chemist achieves the most accurate results with the minimal amount of effort.

The air we breathe is only 21.5 percent oxygen. Most of it is nitrogen (78 percent) and the remaining 0.5 percent is argon and other gases.

The element argon is the most abundant gas in our atmosphere. Even though there's much more helium and hydrogen gas in the universe, only argon is heavy enough to stay in the earth's atmosphere, owing to the force of gravity.

A "cardamist" is the chemical name given to any explosive liquid with a sweet burning taste, such as nitroglycerin.

Before a 1938 revision of the periodic table of elements, the element astatine was called "alabamine" because it was discovered in the state of Alabama.

From the 1500s to the 1700s, tobacco was prescribed by doctors to treat a variety of ailments including headaches, toothaches, arthritis, and bad breath.

De-icing roads and highways in America uses up about 10 percent of all the salt mined in the world.

All U.S. coins are alloys and always contain some amount of copper.

The most abundant metal in the Earth's crust is aluminum. But aluminum isn't found as a free metal in its natural state. Instead, it combines with over 270 different minerals, such as bauxite and silicon. This makes extracting it very difficult and expensive.

Western civilization didn't discover aluminum until 1827. Until it became possible to mass-produce it in the mid-19th century, it was considered a precious metal and used to make expensive jewelry.

The Chinese mined and utilized a crude form of aluminum as early as A.D. 300.

A dash of chromium keeps steel from corroding, and some cobalt turns steel into a permanent magnet.

CHEMICAL COLOR PALETTE

To color fireworks red, a small amount of the metal strontium is added. Barium salts burn green to yellow-green, potassium salts produce violet flames, and copper compounds produce blue, turquoise, or emerald flames. The metal magnesium is used to create a brilliant white burn.

Pure chlorine (Cl) doesn't exist in nature. Natural chlorine is found only in combination with other minerals, including sodium, to make sea salt (NaCl).

Nitroglycerine is made of large, unstable molecules that, when agitated, break into smaller, stable molecules. This breaking up of large molecules into smaller ones releases energy in the form of a heat explosion.

Nitroglycerine can be used to treat heart attacks because inhaling it causes blood vessels to widen or dilate.

Ginger has been clinically demonstrated to work twice as well as prescription drugs for fighting motion sickness, with no side effects.

Seawater, loaded with mineral salts, weighs about 1.5 pounds more per cubic foot (24kg more per cubic meter) than fresh water at the same temperature.

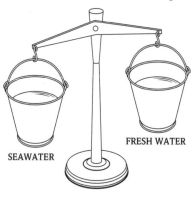

FRESH WATER

SEAWATER

The highest concentration of gold is found in U.S. gold coins, which contain about 90 percent pure gold. Most gold jewelry is made from 18 carat gold and contains about 75 percent pure gold. Finally, dental gold contains only about 50 percent pure gold.

It is estimated that if all the refined gold in the world could be melted down and poured into a single cube, the cube would measure 60 feet (18m) across, for a total of 216,000 cubic feet (64,800 cubic meters).

The term *aqua regia* means "regal water" and refers to a solution of combined acids that dissolves gold. It's one of the few substances that can corrupt this untarnishable metal.

Gold is found in seawater, but no effective process has been designed to extract it from this source.

Most of the world's gold supply comes from South Africa. The rest comes from Russia, Australia, the United States, Canada, Indonesia, Brazil, and India.

Today, gold is painstakingly extracted from quartz, pyrite, and other ores. The ore is crushed to a powder to expose the small gold particles. These are dissolved by adding a cyanide solution. The solution is drained off into a separate container. Finally, zinc powder is added to force the (now purer) gold to solidify again so it can be sifted out and collected.

In ancient Egypt, alchemists tested gold for purity by remelting it and heating it. According to the Papyrus of Leyden, if the gold became whiter, it contained silver. If it became rough and hard, it contained copper or tin. If it softened and turned black, it contained lead.

Because of its softness, pure gold is combined or alloyed with silver, tin, or copper to give it more strength.

Gold is completely impervious to damage by air, water, acids, or bases. This is probably why it was—and is—so highly valued. However, gold can be damaged if submerged in liquid mercury.

Synthesized in 1918, arsenic trichloride, or "butter of arsenic," is a waxy chemical used in the ceramic industry for creating glazes. A stickier liquid form is used to create pesticides for trees and shrubs.

The drinking straw was probably invented by Egyptian brewers to taste fermenting beer without removing the important fermenting ingredients that floated on the top of the container.

THE "ANTIFREEZE" PROTEIN

With few exceptions, animals can't survive being frozen. Ice crystals, formed in the cells, break open the cell membrane and make it impossible for the animal to metabolize when thawed. However, certain species of frog have learned to survive subzero (*Celsius*) temperatures. These frogs make special proteins that prevent the formation of ice (or at least keep the crystals from becoming very large), so that the water in their body tissue remains liquid—a phenomenon known as "supercooling." If you disturb one of these supercooled frogs, even by a light touch, the water in it instantly freezes solid and it dies.

The most abundant atom in living things is hydrogen. About 49.7 percent of the Earth's atoms are hydrogen. Oxygen, carbon, and nitrogen atoms make up about 24.9 percent, 24.9 percent, and 0.3 percent, respectively.

Quinine, historically one of the most important drugs known to man, is obtained from the dried bark of the cinchona tree native to South America. Quinine, which people used before aspirin was discovered, was sold in powdered form in the 19th century.

At room temperature, one element conducts electricity better than any other—silver (Ag).

Slag dumps in Asia Minor and on islands in the Aegean Sea indicate that humans learned to separate silver from lead as early as 3000 B.C.

A solution of silver and iodide (AgI) is used to seed clouds in order to produce rain.

The element fluorine is one of the most corrosive of all the elements. Combined with lead and warmed, it becomes a milky white liquid, called *diamond ink*, that is used to etch glass.

The smallest object ever weighed was a 22-femtogram graphite speck. It was placed on the end of a microscopic tube that was then electrified. The frequency of oscillation of the tube with the speck attached allowed scientists to precisely determine the speck's mass.

The 1938 edition of the periodic table of elements lists "virginium" as an element. The element was named for the state of Virginia and had the symbol Va. The element was later renamed francium.

SIMPLE TECHNIQUES?

Using relatively simple techniques found in unclassified literature, it is possible for almost anyone to make a 1-kiloton bomb as powerful as the one that devastated Nagasaki in World War II. Thankfully, obtaining the 2.2–6.6 pounds (1–3kg) of pure plutonium necessary for the nuclear reaction is much more challenging.

According to the U.S. Natural Resources Defense Council, the can containing a soft drink can hold enough plutonium to make up to six bombs, capable of destroying 40 city blocks.

SPECIAL GLASSES

Because of the danger of ultraviolet light from acetylene torches and burners, glassblowers wear special glasses that contain the elements neodymium and praseodymium. These elements have proved to be effective absorbers of UV rays.

The emerald gem is actually a form of beryl (crystal aluminum) that contains the metal chromium. The ruby is another form of crystal aluminum called a corundum.

The green coating that covers copper objects is a salt called copper carbonate. The salt forms as the copper reacts to moisture in the air.

Adding the metal zirconium to steel creates flint—a metal that sparks when struck or rubbed.

Combining titanium with steel makes the steel less brittle; adding tantalum makes it harder.

Rice paper isn't made from rice but from the small "rice paper tree" (*Tetrapanax papyriferum*) that grows in China and Japan.

Apples are more efficient than caffeine in waking you up in the morning. The apples contain a form of fructose that's particularly effective for alertness.

Banana oil doesn't come from bananas but from petroleum.

Pumice is a stone so porous that it floats in water.

Magnetic iron (magnetite) is produced from iron by the metabolism of tiny bacteria that live in iron ore. Living without light or air, these bacteria eat the ore, which then undergoes a molecular transformation and is excreted as magnetite.

4

Space is a weird place. And people who study space can be a pretty bizarre lot themselves. Here's a collection of oddness from the outer regions.

Our galaxy is so wide that, at the speed of light, it would take you 100,000 years to cross it.

A meteorite the size of a school bus would destroy the entire Eastern seaboard of the United States.

WEIGHTLESS WOES

In space, astronauts can't cry because it's impossible for tears to flow without gravity. Weightlessness also inhibits the natural lubrication of the nasal passages, the quantity of saliva produced in the mouth, and digestive juices in the stomach, and removes the isometric tension of muscles so that arms and legs grow weak. But the most serious problem involves the loss of bone mass. Without gravity, bones become porous and brittle, and are easy to break.

The volume of the Earth's moon is the same as the volume of the Pacific Ocean.

A solar flare is basically a gigantic magnetic arch—like a horseshoe magnet—that attracts itself inward, back to the surface of the sun.

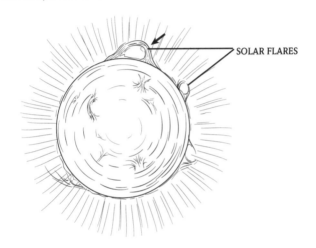

SOLAR FLARES

A solar flare, ejected from the Sun's surface, can reach speeds of 190 miles (306km) per second.

The famous Halley's Comet returns every 76 years. It last appeared in 1986. It appears again in 2062.

Comets originate from a mysterious region beyond the planets called the Oort Cloud, a giant halo that surrounds our solar system and is about 2 light years away from the farthest planet, Pluto.

Although a comet's tail can reach 93 million miles (150 million km) in length, the total amount of gas and vapor it emits would fit into the trunk of a car.

Astronomers suspect that the asteroid belt between Mars and Jupiter is the remains of a planet that either failed to form or was torn apart by the enormous gravitational pull of Jupiter.

The most distant objects in the known universe are quasars: stars that send out powerful radio waves. Because their distance makes them so ancient, quasars provide astronomers with extremely valuable information about the birth of the universe.

Astronauts are not allowed to eat beans before they go into space because the methane gas released while passing wind can damage spacesuit material.

February 1865 is the only month in recorded history not to have a full moon.

It takes three minutes for the sunlight that is reflected from the moon to reach our eyes.

Some astronomers believe that Earth's oceans were formed by water vapor from the tails of passing comets.

A galaxy formation called a globular cluster may contain more than 10,000 stars across only 100 light years. This would make it 50 times denser than our own galaxy.

A light year—the distance light travels in one year—is 5,870,000,000,000 miles (9.45 trillion km).

SATELLITE FACTS

Most satellites orbit the Earth at a height of 93 miles (150km), although some military satellites fly as low as 31 miles (50km)—low enough to burn up in the Earth's atmosphere after only a few weeks. Satellites used for communications and meteorology orbit much higher—at 22,300 miles (36,000km). At this distance, the satellites follow the rotation of the Earth, so they stay in the same position relative to the Earth's surface.

Earth orbits the sun at about 67,000 miles (107,200 km) per hour.

Earth is the only planet not named for a Roman god.

It takes the light from the sun about eight minutes to reach Earth. If the sun exploded this very minute, we would have about the same amount of time before total annihilation.

At 60 degrees south latitude, you can sail completely around the world.

If you were to drive a car at 60 miles (100km) an hour toward the sun for 24 hours a day, you would reach the sun in about 177 years.

Earth tilts on its axis at 23.5 degrees, and this tilt is what causes the seasons, not the distance of Earth from the sun. In fact, during the summer months in the northern hemisphere, Earth is actually farther from the sun than during the winter.

Earth's density is five and a half times that of water. The next densest planet is Mercury, with a little over four times the density of water.

The diameter of Earth is 7,900 miles (12,700km). This makes it the fifth largest plant after the giant planets Jupiter, Saturn, Uranus, and Neptune.

THE LIGHT-GATHERING POWER OF TELESCOPES

A telescope's LGP refers to its light-gathering power, which is many times greater than that of the human eye. LGP is determined by dividing the area of the objective (main lens or mirror) by the area of the human eye. The LGP increases exponentially as the objective increases so that, while a 1-inch (2.5cm) objective has 25 times more light-gathering ability than the eye, a 6-inch (15cm) objective has 900 times the ability.

The refracting telescope as we know it today was invented in 1608 by the German lens maker Hans Lipperhey. He applied for and received a patent for his invention—described as "a device for seeing faraway things as though nearby"—from the Hague in October of that year.

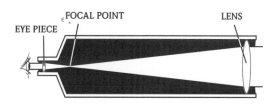

The mirror of the Palomar Observatory telescope in San Diego is 200 inches (500cm) in diameter, 27 inches (67.5cm) thick, and weighs over 14 tons. The telescope gathers 640,000 times as much light as the human eye. The telescope was shipped by rail from the Corning Glass factory in New York and took more than one year to reach San Diego.

GALILEO'S TELESCOPE

Although lenses for magnification existed in Europe as early as the 13th century, the first serious astronomical use of a telescope was in 1609 by the Italian astronomer Galileo. It had a magnification power of about 20. Through this relatively primitive instrument, Galileo was able to make detailed drawings of the surface of the moon and discover four satellites of Jupiter.

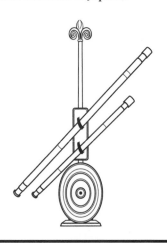

Galileo got into trouble with the Inquisition for his theories, and spent some time in prison.

WHAT IS MAGNIFICATION POWER?

You can calculate the magnification power of a telescope—its ability to make things appear larger—by dividing the focal length of the telescope's objective, or main lens, by the focal length of the telescope's eyepiece lens. For example, a 25-inch (63.5cm) objective focal length divided by a 2.5-inch (6.35cm) eyepiece focal length would give you a telescope with a magnification power of 10.

Stars are divided into six color classifications: red stars are the coolest and bluish ones the hottest.

Next to the sun, the closest star is *Proxima Centauri*, at a distance of 4.23 light years. If you could travel at a speed of 31,000 miles (50,000km) per hour, it would take 88,000 years to get there.

The distance of even the nearest star far exceeds our eyes' ability to resolve it into a distinct object. So when we look at a star, we're actually seeing a snowflake pattern of light created by our eyes.

In space, stars burn with a steady light. The twinkle of starlight is cause by the turbulence of the Earth's atmosphere.

The term *nova* refers to a sudden, and often unexplained, increase in a star's brightness. Stars that become novas often return to their regular luminosity after a period of time.

Absolute magnitude refers to the brightness any star would have if it were placed exactly 10 parsecs from the observer. A parsec is one of the largest measurement units for astronomical distance—equal to 19.2 million miles (30.9 million km).

Astronomers have recorded stars with a brightness, or magnitude, nearly 1 million times greater than our sun.

A pulsar is so named because it "pulses" out radio signals from its core. The first pulsar was discovered in 1967.

Planets are classified into two types: gaseous, like Saturn, Uranus, and Jupiter; and terrestrial, like Earth. Of the terrestrial worlds, Earth is the largest, followed by Mercury, Venus, and Mars.

The zodiacal light, sometimes called the "false dawn," refers to a triangular-shaped glow in the sky that occurs near the eastern horizon about two hours before sunrise. The glow is created by large, widely dispersed dust particles in space reflecting the light of the sun.

The *gegenschein* (counter-glow) is a faint glow that can be seen on a moonless night along the daytime path, or elliptic, of the sun. The glow is caused by large dust particles in space that reflect the sun's light. It was first noticed by the Danish astronomer Theodor Brorsen in 1854.

Crepuscular rays are those beautiful sunbeams that shine down through the clouds.

The northern lights are called the *Aurora Borealis*; the southern lights are called the *Aurora Australis*.

Easter is always the first Sunday after the vernal equinox (when day and night are of equal length) and the subsequent full moon. The equinox is usually March 21, but it can also occur on other days.

The sun is composed entirely of gases and is only about half as dense as water.

The sun emits a steady stream of charged particles from its surface. This "solar wind" can be used to push a spacecraft.

The sun's solar wind enters Earth's atmosphere through holes in our magnetic field near the poles. The particles ignite as they fall to Earth and create the phenomena of the Aurora Borealis (Southpole) and Aurora Australis (Northpole).

The diameter of the sun is about 860,000 miles (1,384,000km).

If the sun were the size of the period in this sentence, the nearest star—*Proxima Centauri*—would be another period, 10 miles (16km) away.

The 11-year sunspot cycle is part of a larger 22-year cycle. During this time the magnetic field of the sun may completely reverse itself.

The gases in a sunspot average 3,000°F (1,649°C) —cooler than the rest of the sun.

The dark center of a sunspot, called the umbra, varies from just a few hundred to over 50,000 miles (80,000km) across.

HOW COLD IS SPACE?

If you could measure the temperature in a deserted region of space, it would be about 2.7 degrees Kelvin (–454 degrees Fahrenheit). Zero degrees Kelvin is "absolute zero," the temperature at which molecules have no kinetic energy and stand completely still. The reason space is a few degrees warmer than absolute zero is because of microwave radiation left over from the original "Big Bang."

Every exploded star, or nebula, contains the seeds of a new star. This seed is called the protostar.

Each square yard on the sun's surface sends out enough energy to power 700 cars, but only about two-billionths of this energy reaches the Earth's surface.

The sun rotates on its axis about once a month.

The surface temperature of the sun is around 10,000 degrees Fahrenheit (5,538 degrees Celsius). However, earth lightning is over five times hotter—about 50,000 degrees Fahrenheit (27,760 Celsius).

The sun is moving at about 12 miles (19km) per second towards the constellation Hercules.

A solar eclipse occurs when the moon is directly between the sun and Earth. The moon's shadow falls on Earth's surface and obscures the sun, either partially or totally, depending on the location of the observer.

A lunar eclipse occurs when Earth is directly between the sun and moon. The shadow of Earth on the moon's surface obscures the moon's reflected sunlight.

During a solar eclipse, the disk of the moon fits neatly over the disk of the sun. This is because the sun is 400 times farther away from Earth than the moon.

Astronomers gather important data about Earth's atmosphere by studying Earth's shadow on the moon during a lunar eclipse.

That ring around the moon you see on a frosty night is caused by ice particles in Earth's atmosphere. Very fine and diffuse particles can cause a huge ring, or even a double ring.

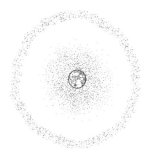

The moon's gravity is about one-sixth of Earth's. If you weigh 170 pounds (77kg) on Earth, you would weigh 28.3 pounds (12.8kg) on the moon.

The moon is approximately 234,000 miles (376,600 km) from Earth.

The moon is moving away from the Earth at a little more than an inch (3cm) per year.

During the six lunar missions from 1969 to 1972, twelve humans have walked on the moon, returning with over 840 pounds (381kg) of lunar rocks.

The highest ocean tides—caused by the pull of lunar gravity—are called *spring tides*. When the tides are at their lowest, they're *neap tides*.

In a sword duel with one of his students over a math problem, the 16th century astronomer Tycho Brahe lost his nose and wore a silver replacement nose for the rest of his life.

ARE WE ALL ALIENS?

Scientists have come to understand in recent years that an enormous amount of material has been exchanged between Earth and extraterrestrial sources such as moons, asteroids, comets, and planets. Some scientists theorize that living microbes could survive the trip through space and perhaps even thrive on our planet. Since the origin of life on Earth is still a mystery, new theories suggest that our planet might have been "seeded" with alien life forms, which over the course of several million years evolved into humans. These theories suggest that we could all be the descendants of space travelers!

The only inanimate symbol in the zodiac is Libra, the scales.

An object that streaks the sky with light and burns up in the atmosphere is called a meteor.

An extraterrestrial object that hits the ground and survives is called a meteorite.

An object that drifts in space before hitting our atmosphere (if it ever does) is called a meteoroid.

Astronomers classify meteorites into three major types: iron, stone, and stony iron. These types have many subcategories.

RED AND BLUE STAR SHIFTS

Astronomers can determine if stars are moving away from us, and how fast, by noting the color of the light they produce in a spectrometer. A "red shift" indicates motion away, since the light waves are stretched into longer wavelengths of red and orange. A "blue shift" reveals motion towards us, as light waves are compressed into shorter wavelengths of blue and violet.

A ring of ice and rock orbits the sun beyond the planet Neptune. Called the Kuiper Belt, astronomers believe that it's the remains of debris that clumped together to form the solar system 5 billion years ago. The new planet, Quaoar (see page 123), was discovered in the Kuiper belt.

Most meteorites come from the asteroid belt, others come from the moon, Mars, and from comets.

FATHER OF METEORITICS

The astronomer Harvey H. Nininger is considered the "Father of Meteoritics." He was the first to do an extensive study of Arizona's Meteor Crater in 1939. His discovery of *silica bombs* and *shocked quartz* at the site proved that the crater was formed by impact and not by volcanic activity. Nininger was also the first to use the then novel metal detector to find iron meteorites.

Meteorites are one of the most valuable sources of information about the formation of the early solar system.

The biggest meterorite recovered so far is the Hoba, Namibia, meterorite that weighs around 60 tons and is about 10 feet (3m) in diameter.

Meteor Crater, Arizona, is the best preserved crater in the world, created about 500,000 years ago. The crater is 150 feet (45m) in diameter, and was originally 700 feet (210m) deep. Silt from the past 500,000 years has filled in about 100 feet (30m).

Most meteors and meteoroids are no bigger than a pea.

About 4 billion years ago, a 100-kilometer-wide (62-mile-wide) asteroid struck Mercury, creating an impact crater that is 808 miles (1,300km) wide. The Caloris Basin, as the crater is called, could hold the entire state of Texas.

Mercury has the fastest orbit of any planet in the solar system, completing one revolution around the sun in 88 days.

Because of Mercury's rate of rotation and its unusual orbit, the sun appears to rise briefly, set, and then rise again before it travels westward across the sky. Then, at sunset, the sun appears to set, rise again briefly, and then set again.

Mercury has the greatest temperature range of any planet in our solar system. The side facing the sun reaches 800 degrees Fahrenheit (427 degrees Celsius)—hot enough to melt tin. The night side temperature drops to –361 degrees Fahrenheit (–218 degrees Celsius).

Astronomers estimate that 80 percent of Mercury's core is iron-nickel, compared with Earth's 32 percent.

Mercury has a very thin atmosphere composed of helium atoms captured from the solar wind.

The pressure on the surface of Venus is equal to 94 Earth atmospheres.

The evening star is actually a planet, usually Mercury or Venus, seen in the west just after sunset.

Often referred to as Earth's sister planet, Venus comes very close to Earth in size and total mass.

Venus is the hottest planet in the solar system. Its dense atmosphere creats a greenhouse effect on the surface of the planet where temperatures reach 860 degrees Fahrenheit (460 degrees Celsius)—hot enough to melt lead!

Venera 14 explorer landed on Venus in 1982 and transmitted photographs that showed a blackened, coal-like surface. After only 54 minutes, the spacecraft was destroyed by the heat.

Martian "canals" were first reported in 1877 by the astronomer Giovanni Schiaparelli. But the effect was actually an illusion. Schiaparelli's crude telescope made for fuzzy images that caused him to "see" things that didn't exist, like canals.

MARTIAN NANOBACTERIA

In August of 1996, NASA and a Stanford University research team announced that they had discovered the fossilized remains of ancient bacterial life inside a Martian meteorite. The meteorite, named Allan Hills 84001 (ALH84001), was found in Antarctica in 1984. Its Martian origin was confirmed by matching trapped gases inside the meteorite with Martian atmospheric data brought back by the Viking spacecraft. The fossil-like structures ranged in size from about 0.4 micron worm-like shapes down to 0.04 micron ovoids. There were also tubular and ball-like structures, all smaller than the smallest bacterial cell known to exist on Earth. Current scientific evidence suggests that nothing can be truly alive and be packed into a body smaller than about 0.2 microns—or 200 nanometers—in diameter. If this is true, then many of the structures scientists found in ALH84001 are too small to have been living cells, but a debate about this continues.

According to one astronomical theory, one billion years ago, an asteroid struck Mars, vaporizing much of its carbon dioxide frost and water ice.

Water may still flow on Mars—underground! A new study of Pathfinder photos suggests that erosion patterns at the sides of craters show recent water activity.

Data gathered by the Pathfinder mission to Mars suggests that the planet was once flooded over thousands of miles of its surface.

The red color of Mars is created by iron oxides, or common rust.

On August 27, 2003, Mars and Earth were a mere 34,649,589 miles (55,785,838km) apart—their closest proximity in recorded history.

A Martian day lasts 24 hours, 37 minutes, and 23 seconds. An Earth day lasts 23 hours, 56 minutes, and 4 seconds.

Jupiter makes one complete rotation around its axis every 9 hours and 55 minutes. Earth rotates around its axis once every 23 hours and 56 minutes.

The surface gravity of Jupiter is 2.6 times greater than that of Earth. A person weighing 170 pounds (77kg) would tip the scales at 442 pounds (200kg) on Jupiter.

Jupiter radiates about 6 times more heat than it absorbs, which bolsters the theory that the giant planet is actually a star that failed to fully ignite.

Saturn has five major ring systems, each of which is divided into thousands of individual ringlets. The ringlets are only about 6.2 inches (15.7cm) thick.

SPOKES IN THE RINGS OF SATURN

When Voyager I passed Saturn, the spacecraft returned photographs that revealed many surprises about its rings. One of them was the discovery that some of the rings are more like "spokes" because they stick out from the planet. Another photograph revealed that some of the smaller rings were twisted into braids that never untangle.

Photographic evidence from the Voyager spacecraft also suggests that Saturn's rings are composed mostly of ice crystals.

Saturn has the lowest density of any planet or satellite in the solar system. In practical terms, you might describe Saturn as the least "solid" of all the planets. For example, if Earth were made of iron and Jupiter of wood, Saturn would be a feather pillow!

Saturn radiates more heat than it absorbs. Astronomers call these planets "gassy giants."

The space between the two largest ring systems of Saturn is called the Cassini Division after Giovanni Cassini, the astronomer who discovered them in the 17th century. Cassini also discovered four moons of Saturn: Iapetus (1671), Rhea (1672), Dione (1684), and Tethys (1684).

Uranus has 15 "regular" moons that travel in predictable orbits around the planet. The remaining six moons are considered "irregular," because they take odd courses and are thought to be the remnants of a collision between Uranus and a large asteroid.

All the moons of the solar system take their names from Greek and Roman mythology, except for Uranus, whose moons are named after Shakespearean characters.

The planet with the most moons is Uranus. At last count, astronomers had named 21. The last moon was discovered in 2001.

Uranus is unique in the solar system because it tips to the side. This means that the planet's north and south poles are found near its equator.

Because of the unusual equatorial position of Uranus's poles, the seasons are extreme. When the sun rises over Uranus's north pole, it stays up for 42 Earth years. When the sun sets, the pole is in complete darkness for the same amount of time.

One of Neptune's 11 moons is larger than the planet Pluto. The moon, Triton, also has a nitrogen atmosphere and rotates in the opposite direction from Neptune's other moons.

True to its name, suggesting the sea, the planet Neptune has a deep blue atmosphere that resembles Earth's oceans from outer space.

Like Jupiter, Neptune has a great dark spot that is probably a huge storm in its upper atmosphere.

Neptune has three rings encircling it. The rings are made from ice particles and rock.

Neptune was discovered in 1846 by first observing the strange behavior of Uranus. Astronomers noticed that Uranus's orbit "wobbled," which suggested the gravitational pull of some other large planetary mass close by.

IS PLUTO REALLY A PLANET?

Astronomers are currently debating whether Pluto is actually a planet at all. In recent years, about 30 enormous asteroids have been discovered just beyond Pluto's orbit, in the disk-shaped cloud called the Kuiper Belt. Since many of these asteroids are nearly as large as Pluto, and nearly as spherical, the classification of Pluto as a planet has been questioned. The pro-planet astronomers point to the fact that, unlike an asteroid, Pluto has distinct terrestrial planetary features and is massive enough to have its own field of gravity.

Pluto is about the size of the United States.

Relative to its size, Pluto has the largest moon in the solar system. Named Charon, it's nearly half as large as Pluto.

Owing to its extremely irregular elliptical orbit around the sun, Pluto was closer to the sun than Neptune was between 1979 and 1999.

NEW PLANET DISCOVERED

On June 4, 2002, astronomers Michael Brown and Chadwick Trujillo discovered a new planet one and a half billion kilometers beyond Pluto. The planet, given the temporary name of Quaoar, is the biggest find in the solar system since Pluto was discovered in 1930. Quaoar is about one-tenth the diameter of Earth and circles the sun every 288 years.

Before digital computers, scientists had to calculate orbits of astronomical bodies by hand, often finding themselves using figures up to nine digits long.

5

Although quiet and unassuming, plants can lead pretty exciting lives. Hold onto your hat for some strange news about the mostly green things.

A notch in a tree will remain the same distance from the ground even though the tree grows taller.

At 167 calories per 3.5 ounces (100g), avocados have the highest number of calories of any fruit.

The "miner lettuce" flower got its name because it was a dietary staple of the forty-niners during California's gold rush days.

Grass, corn, and wheat are all pollinated by the wind. These plants produce a great quantity of pollen, do not need to attract a pollinator, and so conserve energy by not producing flowers.

The herb coltsfoot, also called "British Tobacco," is so salty it can be used as a substitute for mineral salt.

A cucumber is 96 percent water.

The foxglove plant can help prevent congestive heart failure.

The dye from an indigo plant is blue, not purple.

Plants and trees have a ring of tubes called the xylem, which conducts water upward into the leaves.

The rings you see in a tree stump are clusters of xylem tubes. Plants and trees also have a ring of tubes called the phloem, which conducts nourishing sugars throughout the plant tissue.

The wood of a black gum tree is so flexible that you can't break off a twig, but must cut it.

Oak trees do not have acorns until they are 50 years old or older.

EXPLODING APHIDS

The aphid seeks out the sugar solution in trees by boring through the soft tissue and tapping into the phloem tubes that carry the sugar. But since the phloem tubes are pressurized, the sugar sometimes rushes into the aphid's body with such force that it either explodes the little insect or rushes out its posterior. That sticky stuff you find all over your car after you've left it under a tree for a few hours is just that—an aphid accident!

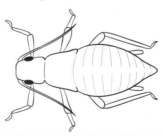

Watercress grows almost everywhere in the world where fresh water runs.

The cellulose in celery (mostly in its stringy fibers) is impossible for humans to digest. Most of the celery passes right through your digestive tract.

The roots of the marshmallow plant were the original source of the spongy confection, which is now made from sugar and gelatin.

The North American phantom orchid is completely devoid of chlorophyll. Its whiteness has only the slightest hint of color—a pale spot of yellow at the tip of each flower.

Pollen is considered the "male" part of a plant's reproductive system.

No species of wild plant produces a flower or blossom that is absolutely black, and so far, none has been developed artificially.

EVOLVING ATTRACTIONS

Flowers evolved scents to attract pollinators, and particular scents developed to attract specific animals or insects.

Sweet, fruity scents attract hummingbirds, while rotten or decaying flesh scents attract flies and beetles.

Color also has this function, with red attracting hummingbirds and purplish-blue attracting bees.

White and pale yellow flowers are easier to see in dim light and so attract moths, as well as flies and beetles.

Plants that depend on butterflies to pollinate them, such as the poppy or the hibiscus, have large colorful flowers with bold shapes. Both their color and shape make them particularly attractive to butterflies.

Rafflesia flowers can measure three feet (1m) across—the biggest flowers of any plant. The rafflesia has evolved to produce a unique scent—the odor of rotten meat. This trick attracts flies for pollination.

HOT CABBAGE

The winter-blooming skunk cabbage generates such intense heat that it can thaw frozen earth and melt a circle in the snow. The bloom also has a putrid odor that attracts flies and gnats.

The stripes you see on flower petals often function as "runways" for flying insects such as bees, flies, and beetles. In the case of blue or purple flowers, the runways are invisible to our eyes, but plainly visible to the honeybee.

Green light is the least effective light to shine on a green-leafed plant for efficient photosynthesis. Most of the green light reflects off the plant's surface.

That green scum you see covering ponds might actually be a carpet of duckweed—the smallest plant with a complete root, stem, and leaf structure.

Cayenne pepper stimulates the appetite, as do the herbs dill, celery, dandelion, caraway, anise, garlic, leek, mint, tarragon, saffron, and parsley.

The word "herb" is from the old Sanskrit word *bharb*, meaning "to eat."

The sandfood plant, dome-shaped and covered with tiny purple flowers, does not contain chlorophyll and cannot manufacture its own food. By sending out parasitic roots, the sandfood draws nutrients from the root of a host plant.

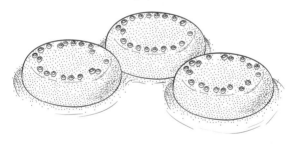

Although it appears parasitic because it attaches itself to trees, the Spanish moss plant uses trees only for support and obtains its water from the moisture in the air.

A lemon will lose 20 percent of its vitamin C after being left at room temperature for eight hours, or in the refrigerator for 24 hours.

The eggplant is a member of the nightshade family, along with the potato and tomato.

The eggplant was originally an Asian ornamental plant whose fruit was thrown away.

The name *eggplant* comes from the early variety that had small, yellow, egg-shaped fruits.

Wheat is the world's most widely cultivated plant; it is grown on every continent except Antarctica.

Hydroponics is the technique by which plants are grown in water without soil.

An uncooked apple is 84 percent water.

BLAME IT ON THE HISTAMINE

Poison ivy and poison oak rashes are caused by the body's intense allergic reaction to a chemical found on the leaves of the plants. This chemical, urushiol, would be nontoxic if the immune system didn't produce the histamines that react to it.

If you wash an area of skin that has been exposed to poison ivy within three minutes after exposure, the urushiol does not have time to penetrate the skin.

The body sometimes "remembers" the areas where poison ivy reactions were most severe. A second exposure to poison ivy can retrigger these original areas—even if the two exposures are years apart!

A "fruit" is any fleshy material covering a seed or seeds.

Botanists define a fruit as the portion of the plant that is part of its reproductive structure. So apples, berries, peaches, peppers, and tomatoes are all fruits. So are watermelons, eggplants, cucumbers, and squashes.

FRUIT OR VEGETABLE?

A rule of thumb for distinguishing fruits from vegetables: For fruits, the seeds are on the inside; for vegetables, the seeds are on the outside.

Botanists (the scientists who study plants) define vegetables as any edible portion of the plant that is not part of its reproductive system. To the botanist, broccoli, spinach, and asparagus are all vegetables.

Botanists describe a nut as an edible seed covered with a hard pericap, or shell. Walnuts and pecans are true nuts. An almond is technically a type of fruit called a *drupe*, because its covering is soft and paper-like. And the peanut, which has a similar soft covering and grows underground, is actually a type of legume.

THE SKINNY ON PLANT FATS

Animal fats such as butter, cheese, and suet are called "saturated" because they contain only single bonds in their molecular structure and are solid at room temperature.

Vegetable fats extracted from olives, canola, and peanuts are called "unsaturated" because they have double bonds in their molecular structure and remain liquid at room temperature.

Unsaturated fats are healthier for us because they have been shown to lower cholesterol levels in the blood.

NO, THE TOMATO IS NOT A FRUIT, SAY THE JUDGES

In 1893 the U.S. Supreme Court defined a fruit as something that either garnishes or concludes a meal. Fruits, at that time, were not subjected to import taxes, and foreign countries could flood the market with lower priced produce. The Court defined vegetables as "plant foods served in, with, or after the soup, fish or meat." Therefore, they declared the tomato was a vegetable and subject to import taxes.

Tomatoes are native to the Americas and were initially cultivated by Aztec Indians as early as A.D. 700.

Tomatoes are a common source of allergies.

The herb peony, when dried and chewed, can help heal a cold sore.

The leaves of the herb betony can work as a natural bandage by helping the blood to clot. The other name for betony is woundwort.

PINEAPPLE WELCOME

In 18th-century New England, pineapples were often brought home by seafarers as gifts. A man bearing a pineapple was a welcome sight, and so the pineapple itself became a symbol of welcome, reproduced in such architectural details as door knockers, column capitals, and fence post ornaments.

Botanists define an herb as "a plant with a fleshy stem, which, after the plant blooms and seeds, dies down to the ground." This isn't a perfect definition, because herbs like sage, thyme, and rosemary have woody stems (although without bark). An addition: the herb should be useful as either a seasoning, medicine, fragrance, or aromatic oil.

Many of the herbs we use today as seasonings were originally medicines. Herbs were kept in apothecary shops (early drug stores) in dried form so they could be used all year. The English word "drug" comes from the Anglo-Saxon word *drigan*, to dry.

In medieval England, "herb" and "vegetable" were the same thing. Later, the herb became the part of the vegetable that grew above ground. For example, the turnip was a vegetable, but its leafy top was called an herb.

Bananas are one of the easiest fruits to digest and trigger very few allergies. This is why they are an ideal food for babies.

Alexander the Great discovered bananas in his conquest of India in 327 B.C.

In eastern Africa you can buy banana beer, which is brewed from fermented bananas.

The riper a banana, the more brown spots it will have on its skin.

A banana is technically an herb because it grows on dense, water-filled leaf stalks that die after the first fruit is produced. Botanists call the banana plant a herbaceous perennial.

TOO DANGEROUS TO EAT

In the United States alone, there are more than 700 species of plants that are dangerous to eat. Among them are some garden favorites such as buttercups, daffodils, lily of the valley, oleander, azalea, bleeding heart, delphinium, and rhododendron.

The lorcel mushroom contains such a powerful poison that even smelling it can cause nausea, dizziness, and severe headaches.

THREE BASIC GROWING CYCLES

There are three basic growing cycles for plants:

*Annuals live for only a year. They start out as seeds, grow flowers, and make their own seeds.

*Biennials live for two years. In the first year they grow from seeds to plants. The plants die in the winter but the roots live and produce new seeding plants in the spring.

*Perennials live for many years. Every winter they store food in their roots, and they grow new foliage each spring.

Because they contain so little water, pecans are the only food that astronauts do not have to dehydrate when flying in space.

It takes a coffee bean five years to yield consumable fruit.

The most widely cultivated and extensively used nut in the world is the almond.

The deadly water hemlock herb belongs to the carrot family. It also goes by the names of spotted cowbane, snakeroot, beaver poison, and death-of-man. Its root contains the lethal poison cicutoxin. The upper part of the plant looks like a harmless artichoke.

The herb rosemary comes from an evergreen shrub that originated in the Mediterranean. It enjoys hot weather and requires little water.

The rose family of plants, in addition to flowers, gives us apples, pears, plums, cherries, almonds, peaches, and apricots.

In the 1920s, inhalable tobacco, or snuff, was so popular in southern Europe that Pope Urban VIII threatened to excommunicate snuff users.

One ragweed plant can release as many as one billion grains of pollen.

Bamboo is the world's tallest grass, sometimes growing to a height of 130 feet (39m) or more.

Plant life in the oceans makes up about 85 percent of all the greenery on Earth.

Tulips were considered so extraordinary and exotic in 17th-century Netherlands that one collector paid 1,000 pounds (454kg) of cheese, four oxen, eight pigs, twelve sheep, a bed, and a suit of clothes for a single bulb of the Viceroy tulip.

Juniper berries smell so strongly of evergreen trees that they have been chewed as a breath-freshener, steeped for tea, ground into a poultice, and made into a jam.

In early 17th-century Europe, tea was so expensive that it was kept in locked metal boxes called cannisters.

The poinsettia plant was brought to the United States in 1828 by Dr. Joel Poinsett, the first U.S. Ambassador to Mexico. The plant, called "flower of the blessed night" in Mexico, was renamed in Poinsett's honor.

The North American plant called the bloodroot was used by the Algonquin Indians as a source of red dye for their faces and bodies. They called it *puccoon*.

The herbs bloodroot, boneset, currant, and magnolia all have fever-reducing properties. Botanists refer to these herbs as antipyretics.

The California redwood, coast redwood, and giant sequoia are the tallest and largest living organisms in the world. However, the oldest living thing in existence is not a California redwood, but a 4,600-year-old bristlecone pine from the White Mountains of California.

In ancient Egypt, the apricot was represented by a series of glyphs meaning "egg of the sun."

SEED STOMPERS

Early Greek and Roman physicians believed that the only way to grow a good crop of basil was to scatter the seeds while cursing and stomping their feet. The belief may have had some merit, since basil seeds germinate quickly when planted far apart under a shallow, hard layer of soil.

The philosopher Pliny the Elder believed that the souls of the dead resided in beans.

Noting his interest in botany, the explorers Lewis and Clark wrote a letter to Thomas Jefferson describing the goldenseal flower. They described it as "a sovereign remedy for sore eyes."

It takes 60 to 75 years for a saguaro cactus (found only in the southwestern United States) to grow branches. Since many saguaros have been destroyed by development and they grow so slowly, these cactuses have become one of America's most precious and highly protected natural resources.

The structure that looks like a salt shaker at the center of a blossom is called the pistil. The pistil is filled with seeds that can sprout for centuries.

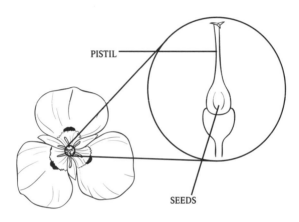

PISTIL

SEEDS

The city of Gilroy, California, still makes the quaint claim that it's the "Garlic Capital of the World." However, Fresno County—the largest agriculture-producing county in the United States—actually produces more garlic.

The wildflower yarrow contains a chemical that speeds blood clotting. According to Greek mythology, the hero Achilles was said to have discovered this property.

MORMON LILY BURGERS

Before the Mormon pioneers learned to cultivate the land around the Great Salt Lake, they survived by eating the tender bulb of the Mariposa lily, just as the Native American Utes and Paiutes had been doing for centuries.

The herb parsley is particularly effective in neutralizing bad breath.

The Chinese called it *jen-shen*, and the American Indians called it *garantoquen*. The name of the plant? Ginseng.

SAINT ANTHONY'S FIRE

The ergot fungus, which infects grain, was responsible for a condition called "Saint Anthony's Fire" in the Middle Ages. Infected grain, even when cooked into bread, caused a burning sensation in the hands and feet; this hallucination was believed to be caused by fire-breathing devils. The condition received its name from the custom of praying to St. Anthony when in the presence of an ergot sufferer.

In the year 857, several thousand people in the Rhine Valley were said to have died from the disease.

As recently as July 1976, nearly all the people in a small French town experienced ergot hallucinations after consuming products from their local bakery.

Willow bark provides the chemical from which aspirin was originally synthesized. The bark has been used as a pain remedy ever since the Greeks discovered its medicinal power nearly 2,500 years ago.

In fruits, the highest concentration of vitamin C is in the pith (skin).

You can recognize a sassafras tree not by the smell of its leaves, but by their variety. On the same tree, one leaf is arrow-shaped, another looks like a mitten, and a third has three segments.

DRINK WATER WITH YOUR MUSHROOMS

Inky Cap mushrooms, found in North American woodlands, are toxic only when consumed with wine or another alcoholic beverage. The poison found in the mushrooms, coprine, reacts with alcohol to produce acetaldehyde—a lethal toxin. This chemical reaction occurs even if the alcohol is consumed days after eating the mushrooms.

HOW HOT IS A PEPPER?

The Scoville Heat Unit Scale was developed in 1912 to measure and compare the heat of chile peppers. Wilbur Scoville, a pharmacist, developed a method that used five tasters. They took exact weights of the peppers, crushed them, and dissolved the capsaicin (the compound that makes peppers hot) in alcohol. The alcohol solution was then diluted with sugar water until the capsaicin was no longer detectable to the palate. If it took 1,000 units of sugar water to one unit of alcohol solution before the capsaicin became undetectable, the sample was said to measure 1,000 Scoville Units. At least three panel members had to agree before a value was assigned. Although this method was the first to measure chile pepper heat, it was imprecise because it involved human testers. Today, liquid chromatography and other sophisticated chemical procedures have replaced the Scoville method.

According to the Scoville method for measuring the heat of chile peppers, the mildest pepper is the bell pepper with an HU (Heat Index) rating of 0. The hottest is the habanero, with an HU of about 100,000.

The substance that gives hot peppers their "bite" is capsaicin, an alcohol-soluble alkaloid compound. Its heat has been shown to interrupt pain signals in nerves when applied to the skin.

Orchids have the smallest seeds. It takes more than 1.25 million seeds to weigh one gram.

6

The workings of our atmosphere are hugely complicated. Even the most powerful super-computers can't tell us for sure whether that picnic planned for next Saturday is a good idea. When it comes to weather, there's just so darn much going on up there! And, like ground fog, this chapter only touches the surface.

The lowest temperature of the day usually occurs right after sunrise.

The term *subsidence* refers to the slow sinking of air usually associated with a high pressure system.

The cooling you feel from the combination of air temperature and wind is called the wind chill factor.

An anemometer is the instrument designed to measure wind speed.

A *zonal wind* flow moves basically from west to east.

The term *radiational cooling* refers to the escape of heat from the earth's surface into space.

The word *pogonip* is of Native American origin and refers to the fog that forms in the mountain valleys of the western United States. A more generic, international term is *upslope fog*.

Fog is most likely to form on a cool, clear night when there's very little wind and a considerable amount of moisture in the atmosphere.

Ground fog is formed when heat radiates from the ground and is suddenly cooled by the air temperature. It's the type of fog we see forming at night and that usually disappears by morning.

Advection fog forms when warm air moves over cool water or ground. The warm air cools to its dew point and creates the kind of thick, ground-hugging fog you can sometimes see from an airplane.

Steam fog forms when cold air moves over warm water. It's the kind of fog that keeps boaters confused and staring at their compasses. The fog forms as the warm water evaporates into the cooler air and increases the air's humidity.

After a rainfall, you can sometimes see *precipitation fog*. This kind of fog forms when the rain evaporates and adds a thick vapor to the air.

Although tornadoes occur worldwide, their greatest concentration is in the United States. About 800 tornados strike the U.S. each year.

Some of the conditions that forecast a tornado include large hail, a dark greenish sky, and a loud roar in the distance from the developing vortex. Wildlife seems mostly unperturbed by developing tornadoes.

The use of radar has allowed meteorologists to predict tornadoes and to decrease the number of injuries and deaths they cause.

A twister can land anywhere. In the late 1980s, one touched down at Yellowstone National Park in the United States, carving a path up the side of a 10,000 foot (3,050m) mountain.

The term *waterspout* refers to a tornado that forms over water. They're usually much weaker than those that form over land, but can become very powerful once they reach shore.

Even more destructive than the tornado itself is the flooding that occurs after a tornado strikes. The flooding is the result of damaged water mains.

TORNADO MEASURING SCALE

The Fujita Scale, named for Ted Fujita at the University of Chicago, is used to measure the intensity of tornadoes. Fujita's scale ranges from F-0 (minor damage) to F-5 (severe destruction).

Tornadoes can form in clusters with several funnels touching down at once. These start out from a storm system called a *supercell*.

Sometimes a "low-pressure explosion" can take place when a tornado suddenly creates a vacuum around a sealed structure. The higher pressure within the structure causes it to explode.

Although 70 percent of all deaths come from F-5 tornadoes, only two percent of tornadoes qualify as F-5. About 69 percent of all tornadoes are F-1 or weaker, and 29 percent are F-2 to F-4.

An F-0 tornado would have just enough force to blow lawn furniture around. An F-5 tornado can lift trains off their tracks. Meteorologists refer to F-5 tornadoes as "the finger of God."

Tornadoes have four distinct stages of formation: organizing, maturing, shrinking, and decaying.

Most of the destruction within the funnel of a tornado occurs as a result of 200 mile (320km) per hour winds and flying debris.

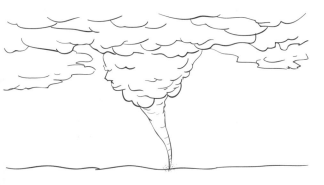

Even though they may form at all hours of the day or night, tornados occur most frequently from 3 P.M. to 6 P.M.

A *wall cloud* refers to the dark, dense cloud that eventually drops a tornado funnel. When the rotation effect of the system is very strong, the wall cloud stretches out around the funnel like a cuff. Meteorologists call this a *collar cloud*.

The unpredictability of the path tornadoes will take gives them the nickname "sidewinders," referring to the movement of some species of snake.

Tornadoes can disappear as soon as they form. This is because the air is very unstable during the various stages of tornado formation, and conditions can shift enough to dissipate a tornado's energy.

Weak F-1 tornadoes can form when a hurricane hits land.

Unlike a tornado, a *dust devil* forms from the ground up and does not involve a weather system.

At any time, 2,000 thunderstorms are occurring around the world, producing lightning that strikes the earth up to 100 times every second.

HOW LIGHTNING FORMS

Lightning forms when rapidly rising air in a thunderstorm crashes into rapidly falling air to create separate positively and negatively charged areas within or surrounding the cloud. Air acts as an insulator, but when the electrical charge is strong enough, the result is a spark we see as lightning. The lightning equalizes the positively and negatively charged areas.

HOW LIGHTNING MOVES

The flash of lightning that appears to hit the ground is actually a series of "strokes" of electrical current. These strokes, occurring about 25 times a second, travel along a pathway that meteorologists call an *ionized channel*.

The channel begins to form when a flow of negatively charged electrons drops from the base of a cloud almost to the ground. At the same time, a short tendril of positively charged electrons moves up from the ground along a tree, metal tower, or tall building.

When the negative flow meets the positive tendril, the channel is complete, and you see the bright strokes of lightning flashing through the channel.

Most lightning travels 10 miles (16km) or less. But depending on other atmospheric conditions, some lightning can travel 20 miles (32km) or more.

Within a lightning bolt, the air is heated to temperatures above 50,000 degrees Fahrenheit (22,760 degrees Celsius)—that's many times hotter than the surface of the sun!

The ancient Greeks and Romans erected temples at sites where lightning stuck. The idea was to worship the gods at these sites in order to appease their anger.

Lightning-detection equipment works by sensing a brief but intense burst of radio energy that comes right before the actual lightning. This energy, called a *sferic*, is what causes the static on your radio immediately before the flash.

Depending on the conductivity of the soil or surface, lightning can spread out in a radius of over 60 feet (18m) from where it first struck.

IN A LIGHTNING STORM

If you're caught outside in a lightning storm, the first thing you need to do is get into a large, completely enclosed space, like a building. If none is available, go into a hard-topped, all-metal vehicle and avoid touching doors and handles. If lightning should strike the vehicle, the current will travel around the car's metal frame to the ground.

If you're in the mountains, your best bet is to get below the tree line and into a grove of smaller trees. You're much more likely to get hit by lightning if you're standing near a tall tree than if you're standing among a few shorter trees. Stay twice as far away from a tree as the tree is tall.

If you find yourself in an open place, crouch on the balls of your feet and wrap your arms as tightly around your body as you can. Making yourself the smallest object around will decrease your chances of getting hit.

Getting struck by lightning can cause poor short-term memory, inability to multitask, distractibility, irritability, and a change in personality—that is, if the victim survives. Many people struck by lightning experience fatal cardiac arrest.

PUT DOWN THAT PHONE!

It's true—talking on the phone during an electrical storm can be dangerous. Along with disconnecting phones, it's a good idea to unplug televisions, computers, and other electrical appliances. Also avoid standing near electrical outlets, showers, and bathtubs until the storm has passed.

Although lightning may look like a powerful source of electrical energy, over half of lightning's energy is lost in the atmosphere in the form of light and electromagnetic waves. This is one of the reasons that harnessing lightning for electrical power would be very difficult.

Lightning can kill several people who are either touching each other or in close physical contact. This ground-spreading lightning is particularly dangerous at sporting events where groups of people sit together on benches.

Lightning kills an average of 73 people in the United States alone each year.

In-cloud lightning jumps from one charged region of a cloud to another. This is the kind of lightning that lights up a cloud like a lantern.

Cloud-to-cloud lightning jumps between oppositely charged clouds and is probably the most frequent type of lightning you see during an electrical storm.

Cloud-to-air lightning leaps from a cloud into the air, never touching the ground or another cloud.

As the name suggests, *cloud-to-ground lightning* stretches from a cloud to the ground—but the actual flash can sometimes travel upward to the cloud base.

Ball lightning is the rarest form of lightning and looks like glowing globes of blue or orange light. The globes can range from the size of a Ping-Pong ball to a sphere several feet in diameter.

Ball lightning lets out a strange hissing sound, followed by a particularly loud thunder clap when the lightning disappears.

Sometimes ball lightning is seen forming around high-current industrial machinery. Hydroelectric plants can often be visited by rolling ball lightning—particularly around large generators—if other atmospheric conditions are right.

SPRITES, ELVES, AND BLUE JETS SIGHTED IN OUTER SPACE

Recently, meteorologists have discovered an interesting form of lightning that leaps from the tops of storm clouds out into space. These so-called sprites, elves, and blue jets were given their names by NASA and first filmed by a space shuttle crew in 1994. The sprites appear to be bright-red

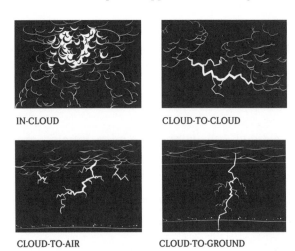

IN-CLOUD

CLOUD-TO-CLOUD

CLOUD-TO-AIR

CLOUD-TO-GROUND

columns of electrified gas that extend about 60 miles (97km) from the tops of storm clouds. At their tops, reddish rings form, which are called elves. Blue jets look like Roman candles that erupt from the tops of clouds and travel up to a height of about 20 miles (32km). They occur at various angles and at speeds ranging from 20 to 60 miles (32 to 97km) per second—faster than the speed of sound, but slower than light or radio waves.

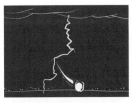

BALL LIGHTNING

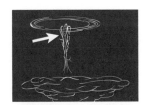

SPRITES

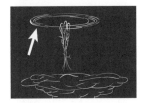

ELVES

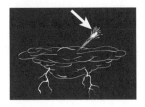

BLUE JETS

Sometimes seen on the ground or traveling along fence edges, ball lightning can be extremely dangerous to livestock or other exposed animals.

To figure out how far away lightning is, count the number of seconds between the flash and the thunder, then divide by five. The resulting number gives you the approximate distance in miles.

Scientists are considering using laser beams to trigger lightning in storm clouds. Controlling the time and location of the lightning strike would allow its energy to be focused and collected in "super batteries."

Thunder is caused when the heat of lightning causes the air to expand very rapidly, creating a shockwave.

During a typical cloudburst, raindrops fall to earth at about 15 to 20 miles (24 to 32km) per hour.

On April 12, 1934, the highest surface wind speed ever recorded occurred over Mount Washington, New Hampshire. It was clocked at 231 miles (372km) per hour.

The *Beaufort Scale* was designed to measure observable wind speed. For example, a wind strong enough to cause a medium-sized flag to unfold slightly from its pole would be called a "fresh breeze" and have a rating of 3.

The term *freshening* refers to an increase in wind strength. The term *moderating* refers to a decrease in strength. The term *veering* refers to a change of wind direction.

The term *backing* refers to a change in the wind's direction without any change in its strength. For example, in the southern hemisphere, winds will start backing when a cold front approaches.

Earth's atmosphere is divided into four parts. From the ground up, they are the troposphere, stratosphere, mesosphere, and thermosphere—the beginning of space.

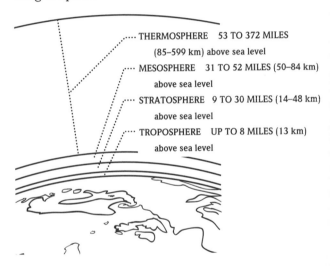

THERMOSPHERE   53 TO 372 MILES (85–599 km) above sea level

MESOSPHERE   31 TO 52 MILES (50–84 km) above sea level

STRATOSPHERE   9 TO 30 MILES (14–48 km) above sea level

TROPOSPHERE   UP TO 8 MILES (13 km) above sea level

A portion of the thermosphere is called the ionosphere, because it contains electrically charged particles, or ions. It is the most important layer for reflecting radio signals back to Earth.

Although air temperature steadily drops as you move up through the troposphere, stratosphere, and mesosphere, it increases in the thermosphere because this layer absorbs much radiation. Temperatures in the thermosphere are known to reach 2,200 degrees Fahrenheit (1,204 degrees Celsius).

HOT AND NOT SO HOT

Certain parts of the world have what meteorologists call a negative heat index. This means that the air is so dry that even a temperature of 100 degrees Fahrenheit (38 degrees Celsius) doesn't feel hot. This is because our bodies keep cool by perspiring. In a negative heat index situation, the body's perspiration rapidly evaporates into the surrounding air, keeping us cool. The opposite of this condition is high humidity. When the air is very moist, even on not-so-hot days, you feel uncomfortable because your perspiration can't evaporate to cool you.

When looking at average worldwide temperatures, the city of Dallol in Ethiopia is the hottest place on earth, at 95 degrees Fahrenheit (35 degrees Celsius).

The coldest place on Earth is Vostok Station, Antarctica, with a mean temperature of –70 degrees Fahrenheit (–57 degrees Celsius).

The higher the altitude, the cooler and drier the air. This simple principle of meteorology has a very complicated name: the *adiabatic lapse rate*.

The driest place on earth is the Atacama Desert in Chile. It receives an average of only 0.004 inches (0.1mm) of rain annually and has recorded 14 consecutive years without rainfall.

Hail falls to earth at a rate of about 70 to 100 miles (112 to 160km) per hour. That's why it's a good idea to stay indoors during a hailstorm!

The path of destruction caused by a hailstorm is called a hail streak.

All hailstones have layers, and each new layer forms when a hailstone is blown back up into the icy upper atmosphere by strong updrafts. When the stone becomes heavy enough, it falls to earth. A golf-ball-sized hailstone needs an updraft of nearly 60 miles (96km) per hour to stay aloft. A baseball-size stone requires a 100 miles (160km) per hour updraft to keep it from falling.

More hail falls in Keriche, Kenya, than anywhere else in the world. In Keriche, it hails an average of 132 days a year!

About 12 percent of the earth's surface is continually covered with snow.

Meteorologists define a blizzard as a weather condition having winds of over 35 miles (56km) per hour for at least three consecutive hours. The visibility has to be less than one-quarter of a mile because of falling or even just blowing snow.

A whiteout occurs in a severe blizzard when blowing snow is impossible to see through. This can be particularly dangerous to pilots attempting to sight-navigate their aircraft.

The wettest place on earth is Cherrapunji, India. Located 4,257 feet (1,298m) above sea level, its annual rainfall is 452.76 inches (11.5m)—fifteen times that of western Europe.

One inch (2.5cm) of rain falling over an area of one acre (0.4 hectares) weighs one ton.

SMOOTH OR BUMPY?

Meteorologists use many different methods to classify clouds. One of the most basic classifications has to do with whether a cloud is smooth or bumpy.

Smooth (stratoform) formations are created by strong horizontal winds and little or no updrafts.

Bumpy (cumuloform) clouds are formed by strong updrafts and little or no horizontal wind. Some clouds, like stratocumulus, combine both characteristics. Stratocumulus clouds are those rib-shaped ones you see in the early morning that usually disappear by noon.

Clouds are all basically the same color. The color variations we see among different clouds have to do with the angle of sunlight, the shadows, the thickness of the cloud, and the size of its water vapor droplets.

Cirrus clouds are among the highest, forming at about 50 miles (80.5 km) above the Earth's surface.

Cirrus clouds, those streaky, wispy shapes that seem to stretch for miles, are the highest-altitude clouds. They're composed mostly of ice crystals.

Meteorologists sometimes refer to Cirrus clouds as "mare's tails," because of their long wispy appearance.

Cirrocumulus clouds are both fluffy and streaky. They never lead to precipitation.

A cumulus cloud would be the most likely formation to create showers that actually reach the ground. Other formations, like stratocumulus, create icy drizzle that evaporates thousands of feet above the earth's surface.

Scarf and cap clouds are smooth cumulus cloud that form around mountains, the result of strong updrafts along the mountainsides.

THE FLUFFINESS FACTOR

Most low-level cumulus clouds have fluffy tops. The reason for this has to do with cooler, drier air at higher elevations. As water vapor—the "stuff" of clouds—moves up through the atmosphere, it enters cooler air. Since cooler air holds less moisture than warmer air, the rising water vapor condenses into tiny droplets that form the foamy "whiteness" of the cloud. An easy way to see this phenomenon is to breathe out on a very cold day. The moisture of your breath can't be absorbed by the cold air and so condenses into droplets: the "cloud" that you exhale.

Cloud names are long. This is why the World Meteorological Organization (WMO) created standard code listings for all clouds. For example:

Ac—Altocumulus	Cs—Cirrostratus
As—Altostratus	Cu—Cumulus
Cb—Cumulonimbus	Fs—Fractostratus
Cc—Cirrocumulus	Ns—Nimbostratus
Ci—Cirrus	Sc—Stratocumulus

Cumulonimbus clouds, the most dangerous—not only because of the precipitation they produce in the form of rain, hail, or snow, but because of their ground-seeking lightning.

ICY ANVIL

A cumulonimbus is a cloud that creates precipitation. It has a ragged bottom because of violent downdrafts, and a fluffy top that can reach as high as the troposphere extends: 9 miles (15km). Sometimes the top of a cumulonimbus cloud punches through the troposphere and into the stratosphere, where it becomes icy and creates a wispy "anvil" shape. The anvil of a cumulonimbus cloud can contain over a million tons of water.

Altocumulus clouds exist above 8,500 feet (2,600m) and form in hot, dry climates. They can create showers, but these are unlikely to reach the ground since the surrounding air is very dry and cool.

FLYING-SAUCER CLOUDS

One of the most beautiful sky objects you can see on a clear day is a lenticular cloud. This smooth "flying saucer" formation is the result of high, strong winds and little upward movement in the atmosphere. You might think of lenticular clouds as "polished" altocumulus clouds. Lenticulars are important to pilots because they can show the existence of dangerous downdrafts along the slopes of mountains. Meteorologists use the initials ACSL for lenticulars. It stands for "altocumulus standing lenticular."

Another way to classify clouds involves measuring the height of the cloud base from sea level. A typical cumulonimbus rain cloud has a base level of about 5,000 feet (1,500m). A midlevel altocumulus floats between 12,000 and 18,000 feet (3,600 and 5,400m). Those wispy cirrostratus clouds drift by at heights of well over 25,000 feet (7,500m).

Clouds

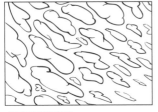

ALTOCUMULUS

CIRROOCUMULUS

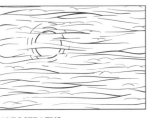

ALTOSTRATUS

CIRRUS

CUMULONIMBUS

CIRROSTRATUS

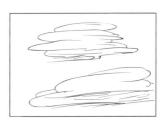

CUMULUS

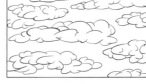

STRATOCUMULUS

FRACTOSTRATUS

LENTICULAR

NIMBOSTRATUS

NOCTILUCENT

A relatively new classification has been invented for a small cloud that exists within the precipitation of a larger, higher cloud. It's called a *fractostratus* of bad weather. These are the dark, ragged clouds that sometimes form under bursting rain clouds.

One of the rarest and oddest cloud formations to be seen are the *noctilucent* clouds. These exist in the thermosphere (up to 372 miles or 600km) above sea level, and are believed to be remnants of comet dust. Look for one just after dusk. You can recognize it by its wispy shape and slight luminosity.

Everyone knows that rain is precipitation in the form of water drops. But to qualify as drizzle, the drops have to have a diameter of less than 0.02 inch (0.5mm).

The wavy line that represents areas of rainfall on a weather map is called an *isohyet*.

The most common type of rain, *frontal rain*, is caused when warm air crashes into cold air, creating what meteorologists call a warm front. The lighter warm air flows over the top of the cooler air. As it rises, it cools and condenses into rain. Frontal rain is the most common type, occurring in most of the world's temperate zones.

Rainfall intensity can be light, moderate, or heavy. For rainfall to qualify as heavy, it must accumulate at a rate greater than one-sixth of an inch (4mm) per hour.

Rain caused by heat rising from the ground is called *convection rain*. This is the kind of sudden shower that happens on a hot day. The ground heat, rising by convection, causes cumulonimbus clouds to form and precipitate.

MOUNTAINS AND RAIN SHADOWS

Relief rain is a type of rain caused by geography. As moist warm air passes over an obstruction such as a mountain, the upward slope of the mountain thrusts the warm air into cold dry air. This creates rain-producing cumulonimbus clouds on the lee side of the mountain. As the air moves over the top of the mountain, it begins to descend and cool, without producing rain. This is why one side of a mountain is often lush and green while the other side is dry. Meteorologists call this drier side a *rain shadow*.

The formation of a tropical cyclone depends on four conditions: a latitude greater than five degrees north or south; a sea surface temperature greater than 79 degrees Fahrenheit (26 degrees Celsius); and a little vertical wind shear to start the whole system rotating.

THE FORCEFUL RAINS OF A MONSOON

Although not exactly a storm, a monsoon is a storm-like weather system that leads to months of constant, heavy rainfall that can result in damaging floods. Monsoon rain is caused by the seasonal rotation of a large air mass covering land and water. During the winter, the sea is warmer than land. This causes the air above the sea to rise and move overland where it cools again. The cooler air moves back over the sea, warms again, and the cycle repeats. During the summer, the cycle reverses. Since the land is warmer than the sea in summer, warm air rises and moves over the sea. Once over the sea, the air cools and picks up moisture. When this cooler, moister air moves back over land, it warms again—but this time the warming leads to the formation of rain clouds, and, eventually, rain. India probably has the best example of a monsoon rain climate.

The violent rain that often precedes a hurricane is called a *storm surge*.

One inch (2.5cm) of rain falling over an area of one acre (0.40 hectares) weighs one ton.

Those cloudlike streamers you see behind high altitude airplanes are called *contrails*.

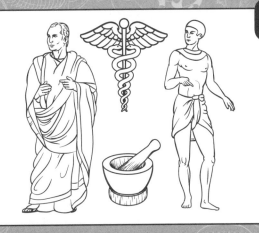

7

ANCIENT MEDICINE

You'd be surprised how much your doctor owes to the likes of Imhotep, Pesheshet, Erasistratos, and Galen. And, at the same time, you'll be delighted to know that medicine has advanced a bit from reading ox livers to diagnose a headache.

Read on to learn more about the strange, fascinating, and chilling medical practices of the toga-and-tunic set.

The first image of a doctor stitching up a wound can be found on the Edwin Smith Papyrus (1600 B.C.).

Ancient Egyptian medicine was considered so advanced that the rulers of neighboring kingdoms would often bribe, cajole, or even send someone to kidnap the Pharaoh's best doctors.

One of the earliest recorded Egyptian medicines was used during the Badarian Age, about 4000 B.C. The medicine was a malachite paste applied to inflamed eyes.

The oldest discovered medical papyrus—the "Kahum Papyrus"—dates from the reign of the Pharoah Amnemhat III, about 1825 BC. It tells how to diagnose pregnancy, treat rashes, and even cure toothaches.

The 3,000-year-old "Ebers Papyrus" was written on a 65-foot (20m) scroll and describes treatments for the eyes, skin, extremities, and organs. It also lists medicinal plants such as mustard, saffron, onions, garlic, thyme, sesame, caraway, and poppy seed, and offers more than 800 recipes for their use.

Ancient Egyptian doctors believed that the body was born in a healthy state and would become ill only when a "foreign agent" entered the body. They believed that the agent took the form of a poison or occult force.

The first known instruction book for surgery dates from 1600 B.C. and was named the "Edwin Smith Papyrus" for its discoverer. It mentions 48 surgeries to the head, neck, shoulders, breast, and chest. It also contains useful information about fractures, which was probably obtained by examining the injuries of pyramid laborers.

The Egyptians made great advances in anatomy and physiology because they embalmed their dead instead of burning them, as was the custom in other ancient cultures.

Egyptian embalmers would empty the contents of the skull by using a long hook that was inserted up the nostrils. In modern medicine, many brain surgeries are performed in the same way.

The Egyptians used honey to keep wounds clean. Honey is a hygroscopic substance, which means that it absorbs water. It also stimulates the production of white blood cells. The Egyptians knew nothing of this—but they did know that applying honey to a wound caused it to heal quicker.

In ancient Egypt, frankincense, date wine, turpentine, and acacia gum were all used as antiseptics.

Applying moldy bread to a wound was first done by the ancient Egyptians. The practice later entered Europe, where it continued through the late 1600s. It wasn't until 1928 that Alexander Fleming extracted penicillin from mold, and 17 years later, was awarded the Nobel Prize.

A collection of 37 surgical instruments is engraved on a wall in the Egyptian temple of Kom-Ombo (2nd century B.C.). Some show amazing similarities to modern surgical instruments and include scalpels, scissors, needles, forceps, lancets, hooks, and pincers.

The Egyptians used opium as crude form of anesthesia when operating on patients. They also created a milder painkiller by mixing water with vinegar and adding ground Memphite stone. The resulting "laughing gas" was inhaled.

Egyptian archeologists have discovered 39 mummies with cancer. Most of these were cancers of the breast and uterus.

Trepanning, or making holes in the skull to relieve brain pressure, was practiced in ancient Egypt. Skulls at the medicine museum in Cairo show circular holes in the frontal bones. New bone growth at the edges suggest that the patients lived through the operations, at least for a few months.

Egyptian doctors treated joint pain by applying ointments containing fat, oil bone marrow, gum, and honey. They sometimes added flour, natron, onion, cumin, flax, frankincense, or pine.

In ancient Egypt, cough was treated by swallowing a mixture of honey, cream, milk, carob, and crushed dates.

In ancient Egypt, a migraine headache was considered a special ailment that called for special treatment. The patient ate siluris (an electric catfish) that was fried slowly in peppered oil.

The word "cataract" comes from the Latin *cataracta,* meaning a downward trickle of water. The Egyptians and Romans believed that cataracts were caused by liquid flowing from the brain into the eyes.

In ancient Egypt, cataracts were treated by applying a mixture of tortoise brain and honey. The Egyptians thought the tortoise brains, along with the sluggish honey, possessed magical properties that would stop the flow of fluids.

The first known surgery for cataracts was performed in the Egyptian city of Alexandria in about A.D. 100.

Ancient Egyptian physicians treated night blindness by mashing an ox liver into a paste and frying it pancake-style. Ox liver is known today to be a rich source of vitamin A, which is important for the health of the eyes.

Some language experts believe that the word chemistry comes from the word "Kemet," the ancient name for Egypt. Maybe this is because the Egyptians were such great mixers of potions!

Some basic Egyptian medicines were made from sulfur, antimony, and zinc, which were ground into powders and used as eye and skin ointments. More than 150 kinds of plants were used, such as senna, sycamore, castor oil, acacia gum, mint, and linseed.

The Egyptians used yeast internally to treat indigestion and externally to treat leg ulcers.

During the time of pyramid building, workers ate lots of radish, garlic, and onion as antibiotics. This was believed to protect them against infectious diseases that could spread rapidly among large groups of people.

In ancient Egypt, skilled doctors were treated as gods. Temples were built to honor Imhotep, the physician of King Zoser of the 3rd dynasty. Imhotep was one of the world's first geniuses, famous as an astronomer and architect.

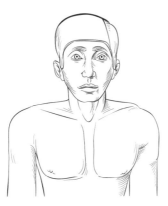

A limestone from the time of Rameses II (1240 B.C.) lists the names of 40 pyramid laborers who "called in sick" over a period of one week.

The first female physician known practiced at the time that the great pyramids were being built (4th dynasty). Her name was Peseshet and she was titled "Lady Overseer of the Lady Physicians." She supervised a corps of women who were qualified physicians, not midwives.

The earliest doctors were often priests, some of whom were later revered as gods.

The ancient Greeks were not "scientific" in the modern sense of the word, especially in the way they practiced medicine. Greek doctors thought they could discover more by reflection and argument than by practice and experiment.

Many of the medicinal herbs we use today were first used by the ancient Egyptians.

The great Greek physician Hippocrates (460–370 B.C.) was the first to separate medicine from philosophy and to ridicule the idea that disease was a punishment for sin.

The world's first true physician, Hippocrates, was scornful of those who practiced philosophy as well as medicine. He wrote that the true doctor should devote himself entirely to treating and curing patients.

Before Hippocrates, much of the traditional treatment for injuries and ailments practiced by the ancient Greeks came from folk medicine.

One of Hippocrates' teachers was Alcmaeon of Croton, who operated on the eye and discovered passages linking the eye to the brain. He was also one of the first to say that the brain was the source of thought and feeling and not a "temperature regulator," which was a widely held belief at the time.

Hippocrates' Theory of the Four Humors stated that good health is a balance between the elements Earth, Water, Fire, and Air. His ideas provided the basis for medical theory up until the 18th century.

The Greek doctor Alcmaeon of Croton believed that good health was a balance among basic forces of the body. These were heat and cold, moisture and dryness, and bitterness and sweetness. Hippocrates took these theories and turned them into his Theory of the Four Humors.

Hippocrates taught doctors that they had no "rights," only "duties." From this teaching came the Hippocratic Oath, which, oddly enough, was not written by Hippocrates.

The original Hippocratic Oath was written by a school of philosophers known as the Pythagoreans and was actually a reaction against the writings of Hippocrates. The Pythagoreans were conservative and even backward-looking in many ways—forbidding many medical practices, including surgery!

The first half of the Hippocratic Oath describes the duties of the pupil towards his teacher and the teacher's responsibility to share his medical knowledge. The second half summarizes a code of medical ethics, much of which does not agree with the true principles and actual practices of Hippocrates.

The ancient Greeks believed that the soul resided in the blood.

The Greek physician Erasistratos accurately described the brain. He correctly distinguished the cerebrum from the cerebellum, and wrote that the brain was the coming together of all the body's nerves.

Erasistratos was the first ancient Greek physician to dispel the popular notion that nerves are hollow and filled with *pneuma*, or air. He also accurately described the heart and circulatory system.

By A.D. 100, medical dissection became a regular practice in the Egyptian city of Alexandria. Before this time, it had been condemned on religious grounds.

Before 200 B.C. there were no doctors in Rome and the professional practice of medicine was unknown. Folk remedies were offered by the head of the household because of his knowledge of the farm and the needs of his livestock.

The Romans considered cabbage to be a magically protective food. The philosopher Cato wrote that Romans should not only eat cabbage at every meal, but also drink the urine of someone who'd eaten cabbage two days before.

Early Roman folk medicine often relied on only one or two remedies that were combined and concocted into ointments, teas, or medicinal foods. The fact that only two ingredients were used puzzles historians. Some believe that the number may have had some superstitious significance.

According to the Roman historian Pliny the Elder, the early Romans believed wool had magical powers. Unwashed wool dipped into a mixture of melted fat was recommended for treating bruises and swellings. Ram's wool, washed in cold water and soaked in olive oil, was used to cure rashes. Wool dipped into a mixture of oil, sulphur, vinegar, pitch, and soda was said to cure aching joints.

The practice of hepatoscopy, or reading divine signals in the livers of animals, was practiced by the Etruscans, ancestors of the Romans. But only state-appointed priests were allowed to do it.

According to Pliny's *Natural Histories*, the first doctor to come to Rome was Arcagathus, who arrived from Greece in 219 B.C. Arcagathus was allowed to become a citizen, and a medical shop was set up at state expense for his use.

Because Arcagathus was an expert wound surgeon, he became popular and famous. But he was an aggressive surgeon whose patients often died. He was finally disgraced and removed from his post with the title "carnifex—the executioner."

In both ancient Greece and Rome, doctors didn't need licenses or any formal training to practice. Anyone could call himself a doctor. If his methods worked, he attracted more patients, if not, he found himself another job.

Medical training in ancient Greece and Rome consisted mostly of apprentice work. Men trained to be doctors by following around another doctor.

In ancient Rome, many doctors were freed Greek slaves, which meant that their social standing was very low.

Greek society accepted the practice of medicine as a profession and paid physicians for their services. But doctors were considered only specialized craftsmen and were allowed neither to mingle with the Greek elite nor to build houses close to ordinary citizens.

During the time of the Roman philosopher Cato (234 B.C.–149 B.C.), the Roman senate passed laws that prevented wealthy Romans from walking about with their private Greek physicians behind them. These laws were designed to keep the rich from showing off and arousing the anger of poorer people.

The Roman writer Plutarch mentions that doctors would do anything to attract patients, including walking potential clients home from a bar and sharing dirty jokes with them.

COMING DOWN WITH A COLD? TRY THIS

The Roman philosopher Cato the Elder (234 B.C.–149 B.C.) suggested the following remedy for both people and livestock:

"If you have reason to fear sickness, give the patient/oxen before they get sick the following remedy: 3 grains of salt, 3 laurel leaves, 3 leek leaves, 3 spikes of leek, 3 cloves of garlic, 3 grains of incense, 3 plants of Sabine herb, 3 leaves of rue, 3 stalks of bryony, 3 white beans, 3 live coals, and 3 pints of wine. You must gather, macerate, and administer all these things while standing, and he who administers the remedy must be fasting. Administer to each ox or to the patient for three days, and divide it in such a way that when you have administered three doses to each, you have used it all. See to it that the patient and the one who administers are both standing, and use a wooden vessel."

ANCIENT DOCTOR JOKES

Because the cure rates of Roman doctors were so low, many Romans ridiculed them. Roman literature is filled with numerous doctor jokes, including the following:

"Until recently, Diaulus was a doctor; now he is an undertaker. He is still doing as an undertaker what he used to do as a doctor." (*Martial, Epigrams 1.47*)

"You are now a gladiator, although until recently you were an ophthalmologist. You did the same thing as a doctor that you do now as a gladiator." (*Martial, Epigrams 8.74*)

"Socles, promising to set Diodorus's crooked back straight, piled three solid stones, each four feet square, on the hunchback's spine. He was crushed and died, but he became straighter than a ruler." (*Greek Anthology XI, 120*)

Instruments found throughout the Roman Empire show that surgery had advanced tremendously. In fact, surgery was probably the greatest contribution the Romans made to the practice of medicine.

Most Roman surgical instruments were made of bronze, or occasionally of silver. Iron was considered taboo by both the Greeks and Romans and so was never used for surgical instruments on religious grounds.

There were no medical services available to Roman soldiers. But Roman officers always brought along their personal Greek physicians to battles.

The Roman philosopher Cicero believed that the herb dittany would cause arrows to fall out of the bodies of wounded soldiers.

Knowledge of Greek medicine was passed on to the medieval world by Claudius Galenus—also known as Galen—who was a Greek writer and physician born in the city of Pergamum (now in Turkey) in A.D. 131.

Galen is known to have written at least 20 books, maybe more, because much of his work was destroyed in a fire in A.D. 199. In addition to general medicine, he wrote about anatomy, physiology, hygiene, embryology, psychiatry, nutrition, and philosophy.

According to Galen, the study of philosophy was an important part of a doctor's training. His work entitled "That the Best Doctor is Also a Philosopher" explains that a doctor must not be motivated by profit and should learn to despise money.

Galen believed that the basic element of life was pneuma (air), which took three forms. The first was animal air (*pneuma physicon*) in the brain; the second was vital air (*pneuma zoticon*) in the heart; and the third was natural air (*pneuma physicon*) in the liver. Galen thought that the liver was the center of nutrition and metabolism.

Galen made many mistakes, but he remained the unchallenged medical authority for over a thousand years. After he died in A.D. 210, serious medical writing stopped, because it was believed that Galen had said everything there was to be said about medicine.

It was reported by his contemporaries that Galen kept at least 20 scribes on hand to jot down his every thought.

Galen's errors persisted for nearly 1500 years until Vesalius, the 16th century Italian anatomist, began to correct them.

The Middle Ages produced no great doctors to take the place of such important figures as Imhotep and Hippocrates in the ancient world.

The first early medieval medical university was founded in the 10th century in Salerno, Italy, where Greek manuscripts written by such physicians as Hippocrates were studied. At the time, this was the only school of healing that allowed female students. It was headed by a woman named Trotula, or "Dam Trot," as she was then known.

In the 10th century, a book of herb recipes appeared called *The Leach Book of Bald*. This book, written by a monk, contained herbal information from the traditions of the Druids in Wales and combined them with Greek and Roman herbal knowledge.

Most medieval medicines were "simples," made of herbal ingredients that were eaten raw or made into teas.

A NASTY-SOUNDING REMEDY

One remedy that apothecaries (whom we now call pharmacists) borrowed from a recipe by the Greek doctor Galen, was called theriac or treacle. It included over 50 ingredients, including the bark of trees and skins of snakes, took 40 days to prepare, and had to "cure" for 12 years! Medieval doctors claimed that treacle cured everything—and most people believed them.

Astrology was important to doctors during the Middle Ages. Astrologers were often called on to forecast the spread of the Black Death.

Several famous female herbalists lived in the 10th and 11th centuries. The most prominent was Hildegard of Bingen (1098–1179), a German nun who composed music that is still performed today.

To treat smallpox, a medieval doctor would arrange red drapery around the patient's bed. This practice may have had a magical reason, or perhaps was an attempt to protect the patient from disturbing light.

In medieval times, thousands of people died from what are treatable diseases today—influenza, measles, pneumonia, scarlet fever, and tuberculosis.

Leprosy was such a serious disease in the Middle Ages that those infected—while in relatively good health—were encouraged to plan and attend their own funerals before the disease disfigured and eventually killed them.

Medieval doctors thought leprosy was extremely contagious, so lepers were not allowed to touch anything except by using a cane. Today we know that, although leprosy can be transmitted from person to person, it is very difficult to catch from touch alone.

Wealthy medieval lepers could live in luxurious leper colonies with their entire families. Many rich medieval men left their fortunes to such colonies, many of which were run by the church.

Medieval doctors believed that serious disease was spread by bad odors and that good odors could protect against infection. During plague times, people wore long beaks filled with fragrant spices to protect them from unwholesome air.

GOOD AND BAD HUMORS

In medieval times, doctors believed that the body was divided into four "humors"—an idea that was borrowed from Hippocrates. Each of the humors had a body fluid associated with it. For example, fire with yellow bile; earth with black bile; water with phlegm; and air with blood. The humors had to be balanced for health. If a person was moody or became ill, the humors had to be balanced by letting out blood or giving a laxative.

Medieval doctors believed that the colors of flowers indicated how useful they were in treating certain diseases. For example, the yellow flowers of dandelion and fennel showed that these plants were good for treating diseases related to "yellow bile" conditions, such as jaundice. These beliefs were written down in a document called the "Doctrine of Signatures."

During medieval times, who provided your medical care depended on your social position. University trained doctors, all men, treated only wealthy patients. Folk healers, usually women, took care of everyone else.

WITCH HUNT?

There was a great deal of hostility among the different "classes" of doctors during the Middle Ages. University-trained physicians hated those who practiced more herbal and "magical" remedies. Some historians have even suggested that the persecution of witches started as an attempt by trained doctors to get rid of the untrained ones.

So you thought that the Earth was just some big, dumb rock spinning its way through space to oblivion, did you? Think again—the Earth is an out-and-out circus of activity. From its erupting volcanoes to its churning tides, there's never a dull moment on the third planet from the sun. Find out more!

Seventy-one percent of Earth's surface is covered in water.

Earth is the only planet where water exists in liquid form at the surface.

Earth has seven continents: Africa, Antarctica, Australia, Asia, Europe, North America, and South America.

The circumference of Earth, measured at the equator, is about 25,000 miles (40,250km). Since Earth bulges slightly at the equator, circumference measurements taken from pole to pole would yield a smaller number.

Although the Earth is about 4.5 billion years old, rocks over 3.5 billion years old are extremely rare.

Scientists estimate that the temperature of Earth's core is about 7,500 degrees Kelvin (13,040.33 degrees Fahrenheit, 7,226.85 degrees Celsius). In comparison, the temperature of the sun is only about 5,800 degrees Kelvin (9,980.33 degrees Fahrenheit, 5,526.85 degrees Celsius).

The Earth's magnetic field is created, in part, by the spinning motion of its molten iron core. The core acts like an electrical generator, creating a magnetic current that encircles our planet.

Once every half-million years, the Earth's magnetic pole completely reverses direction so that the north-attracting pole drifts to the geographic south and the south-attracting pole drifts to the geographic north.

In the past 75 million years, Earth's poles have reversed 171 times.

Any stationary iron object will eventually become magnetized so that it has a distinct north and south "pole." To test this out, hold a compass to a can of soup that has been sitting in your cupboard for a while.

Current research shows that about 900 million years ago, when the Earth's rotational rate was greater than it is now, there were 481 eighteen-hour days in a year.

The moon's gravitation slows down the Earth's rotation by about two milliseconds per century.

Silicon dioxide, or quartz, is one of the most abundant minerals on Earth. It's found in all colors except green.

The semiprecious stones amethyst (purple) and citrine (yellow) are just highly compressed forms of quartz.

The most rare and expensive color of opal is black.

The most rare and valuable diamonds are either pale blue or colorless.

A clue to a diamond's hardness can be found in its molecular structure. Every carbon atom is linked tightly to four other carbon atoms, forming a dense framework.

A diamond exposed to enough radiation will change from clear to yellowish.

Poor-quality diamonds become industrial diamonds. The diamonds are crushed and used to coat heavy-duty cutting instruments.

Synthetic diamonds are made by subjecting graphite to extreme heat and pressure.

The gemstone topaz comes in a variety of colors including yellow, brown, orange, light purple, and "smoke." A blue topaz is rare and highly valued.

THE MOHS SCALE OF MINERAL HARDNESS

To test the hardness of minerals, the German mineralogist Frederich Mohs invented the Mohs Scale in 1812. By using a carefully calibrated scratch test, his scale gave a soft-to-hard rating of familiar minerals from 1 to 10. On the scale, the mineral talc is the softest, with a rating of 1. It's followed by gypsum (2), calcite (3), fluorite (4), apatite (5), feldspar (6), quartz (7), topaz (8), corundum ruby (9), and diamond (10). The scale is only relative. In terms of absolute hardness, diamond is actually four times harder than corundum and six times harder than topaz.

For fun, we can measure other objects on the Mohs Scale, too. For example, the "scratchability" of aluminum foil is 2.5, a penny is 3, glass is 5.5, and a steel file is 6.5.

Green lava stones, or greenstones, are formed when lava comes into contact with seawater. The green color results from the chloride in the water.

Obsidian is a particularly hard and glassy type of lava-formed igneous rock. Its glassiness is the result of to its high basalt content.

The cataclysmic collapse of a volcanic mountain summit, due to an enormous empty chamber beneath it left by spewing lava, creates what geologists call a *caldera*. Over thousands of years, many calderas fill with water. Crater Lake in the state of Oregon is an excellent example of this process.

The term *striations* refers to the scratches a glacier leaves in its path. The scratches are made from rocks caught in the glacier's base. Geologists can determine the direction in which a glacier moved, and even its speed, by studying these scratches.

A beneficial dust called *loess* regularly blows across portions of Europe, Asia, and North America. The dust, made from the deeply churned soil that glaciers leave behind after they melt, is rich and fertile.

Those sharp jagged crests seen at the tops of mountains are called *aretes*.

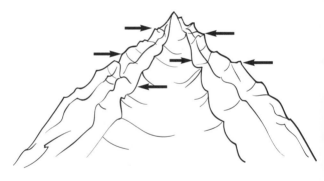

In very windy terrains, piles of pebbles, called *ventifacts*, often collect in the sharp ridges of mountains.

The rocks that accumulate at the foot of a bedrock cliff are called *talus*. Many meteorites are found in talus deposits—particularly in Antarctica.

The term *scree* refers to the steep masses of pebble and debris that accumulate at the bases of mountains. The word comes from the Scandinavian word *skritha*, because the phenomenon was first observed in Scandinavia.

Plutonic rocks describe igneous, or heat-formed, rocks created deep underground. They are named for the Roman god of the underworld, Pluto.

According to geologists, the term *saltation* describes particles of dust suspended in air or water. A dust cloud is an example of saltation, as well as the motion of silt in streams.

Geologists believe that only one huge continent existed 200 million years ago, which eventually broke up into the seven continents we know today. They named it Pangaea.

THE GREENHOUSE EFFECT—ALWAYS BAD?

Because of the modern burning of fossil fuels, too much carbon dioxide has been released into the air, creating global warming. This "Greenhouse Effect" raised the ancient Earth's temperature from a chilly −24 degrees Fahrenheit (−31 degrees Celsius)—at which temperature all the oceans would freeze, to a more livable 57 degrees Fahrenheit (14 degrees Celsius). However, global warming is a serious matter: just a slight temperature increase could melt the polar ice caps and flood Earth.

Antarctica is the highest, driest, coldest, windiest, and emptiest place on earth.

The coldest temperature ever recorded was in Antarctica, at Vostok station. The actual temperature was −128.6 degrees Fahrenheit (−89.2 degrees Celsius).

The highest temperature ever recorded was in Libya, at the Al Aziziyah station. The temperature was 136 degrees Fahrenheit (58 degrees Celsius).

A coral ring, or *atoll*, forms when a volcanic cone—made from spewing lava—rises from the sea. Living coral attach themselves to the base of the cone. Eventually, the volcanic activity stops and the cone begins to sink, leaving a ring of coral behind.

Coral atolls can be found around mountaintops in Alaska. These mountaintops were once volcanic islands.

The Great Barrier Reef, along the continental shelf of northeastern Australia, is the longest coral reef on Earth, measuring about 1,243 miles (2000km).

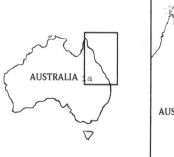

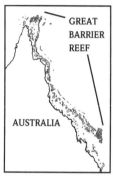

The theory of plate tectonics states that the Earth is covered in huge plates that move as a result of heat currents deep below the surface.

Earthquakes occur when the edges of these plates rub against each other. The rifts and cracks that result are called fault lines. Some of them are more active than others.

Each magnitude level on the Richter scale is a tenfold increase. This means that an earthquake measuring 6 on the Richter scale is 1,000 times stronger than a quake measuring 3 on the scale.

The location of an earthquake underground is called its *focus*. The point directly above the focus on the surface is the epicenter.

PHANTOM CANNONS

Some Earth tremors, too weak to be felt, can nonetheless make a low-pitched booming sound—like a distant cannon—that startles people and animals alike. This is particularly true if the tremors occur near water, where their sound is transmitted more rapidly. Called the Barisal Guns Effect, this phenomenon was named after the city of Barisal, in Bangladesh, where the sounds were first identified.

A *tsunami* is a giant tidal wave caused by earthquake activity. It has nothing to do with the tides. Shortly before a tsunami hits land, it pulls millions of gallons of seawater away from the shore, leaving behind an eerily exposed shelf that may extend hundreds of feet.

The largest tsunami ever recorded was about 210 feet (63m) high, or about 18 stories above sea level. It smashed into Siberia's Kamchatka Peninsula in 1737.

The oldest fossils of living organisms are about 3.5 billion years old.

Fossils can take many forms. Plant or animal parts preserved in shale or glacial ice are called *original remains* because a portion of the original organism exists.

A carbonized fossil is one where the organism itself has vanished, but a perfect cast of it exists in mud or shale. Many delicate plant fossils take this form.

A mineralized fossil refers to animal or plant matter where the soft tissue has been replaced by minerals—frequently calcite, quartz, or pyrite. Carried by groundwater, the minerals seep into the soft tissue, eventually replacing it.

One of the most abundant mineralized fossils found in the United States is the trilobite—a hard-shelled, boneless marine animal that lived more than 500 million years ago, but is now extinct.

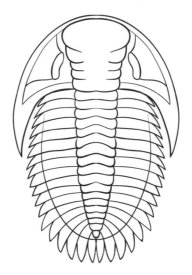

Trilobites roamed the sea floor and coral reefs in search of food.

Unlike other terrestrial planets in our solar system, Earth has only about 120 impact craters on its surface. Water and wind erosion, as well as erupting volcanoes and earthquakes, have erased most of them.

Geologists have identified an 112-mile (180km) diameter crater in Mexico that they believe was formed by a particularly violent meteoritic explosion. The meteorite, estimated to be six miles (9.6km) in diameter, may have contributed to the extinction of the dinosaurs. The crater, named Chixalub (pronounced "sheesh-ah-loob") is estimated to be about 65 million years old.

The largest known impact crater on Earth is the Vredefort Ring in South Africa. It has a diameter of 186 miles (299km) and was formed about 2 billion years ago.

The Marianas Trench, an elongated valley on the floor of the Pacific Ocean, is the deepest depression on Earth. A United States Navy bathyscape reached the bottom in 1960 and measured its depth at 35,798 feet (10,739m).

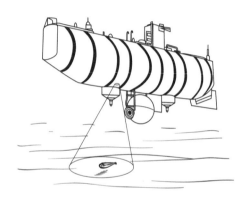

Deep in the Marianas Trench, the temperature of the water is always just above freezing, and the pressure is more than 1000 times what it is on the surface, but many bottom-dwelling fish and invertebrates call it home!

At 29,028 feet (8,708m), Nepal's Mount Everest is the highest land-based mountain (a mountain that sits on dry land and not sea floor) in the world. Formed about 60 million years ago, Everest is named after Sir George Everest, the British surveyor who accurately calculated its height in 1800.

In Nepal, Mount Everest is called Sagarmatha, which means "goddess of the sky."

At 28,259 feet (8,478m), the mountain K2 at the China-Pakistan border is the second highest peak after Mount Everest.

The third highest mountain is Mount McKinley in Alaska—20,320 feet (6,096m) high.

Steam explosions can occur when a cool rain falls on the active volcano Kilauea on Hawaii's big island.

KING OF THE MOUNTAINS

Although Mount Everest, at a height of 29,028 feet (8,848m) is called the tallest land-based mountain, the inactive Hawaiian volcano Mauna Kea is actually taller. Only 13,796 feet (4,205m) of Mauna Kea rises above sea level, yet the mountain is a staggering 33,465 feet (10,200m) tall if measured from the ocean floor. This means that Mauna Kea would be 4,437 feet (1,352m) taller than Mount Everest if they were placed next to each other.

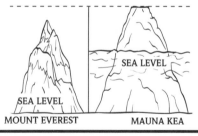

Mauna Kea typically stays snow capped from December to May. Its name in Hawaiian means "White Mountain."

Geologists define dust as particles small enough to be carried by air currents.

Dust is the most widely dispersed terrestrial matter. Dust from the Southwestern United States regularly blows into the New England states.

Dust is important in the formation of rain and snow. Moisture condenses around dust particles so that precipitation can occur.

The dust that collects on clothing can provide detectives with important information about the movement of a crime suspect.

Dust can be combustible. Mixed with the right quantity of air, grain dust can spontaneously explode.

PRESSURE READINGS

Pressure is measured in a unit called an *atmosphere*. One atmosphere equals 14.7 pounds (6.67 kg) on each square inch (6.5 square cm) of surface area.

If you stand on dry land at sea level, you feel the pressure of one atmosphere, or 14.7 pounds (6.7kg) on each square inch of your body. This is the pressure of hundreds of miles of air above you. But if you sink in sea water, which is denser than air, you feel the pressure of a second atmosphere at only 33 feet (9.9m) and the pressure of a third atmosphere at 66 feet (19m). This means that, in addition to the atmosphere you feel on dry land, you gain one atmosphere of pressure for every 33 feet you sink in seawater. So at 66 feet below, you feel the pressure of three atmospheres, or 44.1 pounds (20kg) pressing down on each square inch of your body. In fresh water, you would have to sink 34 feet (10m) to gain an atmosphere. This is because fresh water contains no salt and is therefore lighter than seawater.

Human divers can sustain pressures of up to four atmospheres safely with the proper equipment. Beyond that, submarines are needed.

A *batholith* is a large underground reservoir of solidified lava. One of the largest is the 73,000 square mile (189,000 square km) Coast Range Batholith that straddles Western Canada and Alaska.

Lithostatic pressure refers to pressure exerted equally in all directions, such as what a scuba diver experiences when underwater. It can also refer to the force exerted on a rock buried deep within the Earth by overlying rocks. Because the pressure is equal from all sides, compression makes the rock smaller without changing its shape.

Due to plate movement, the ocean floor is spreading at the rate of a little over an inch (3cm) a year.

Of all the oceans, the Pacific has the greatest average depth—about 14,130 feet (4,307m).

Canada has the largest coastline of any county—56,453 miles (90,852km). This is due to the extensive collection of islands in the north.

With a maximum depth of 5,315 feet (1,594.5m), Lake Baikal in Russia is the deepest lake in the world.

The Mid-Ocean Ridge is Earth's longest mountain range. It circles from the Arctic Ocean to the Atlantic Ocean, passes into the Indian Ocean, and finally joins the Pacific Ocean. It is four times longer than the Andes, Rockies, and Himalayas combined.

Egypt's Nile River is the longest on Earth, measuring 4,160 miles (6,695km) on its northward journey to the Mediterranean Sea.

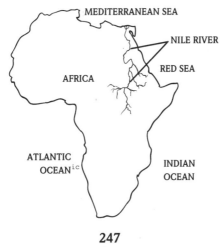

Most icebergs (also called ice islands by geologists) originate in the tidewater glaciers along the west coast of Greenland. There are 20 named glaciers in this area, and as many as 15,000 icebergs will break off from them each year.

All icebergs started as snow that fell more than 15,000 years ago.

ISLAND VERSUS CONTINENT

Geologists distinguish continents from islands not only by their larger size, but by their density. Continents are made up of low-density rock, so they float high on Earth's mantle. High-density islands emerge from volcanic activity deep within Earth's mantle. According to this definition, Greenland is an island; Australia is a continent.

Although no two icebergs are the same, geologists classify them into shapes in order to recognize and log them. Some of the basic shapes are tabular, blocky, wedge, dome, pinnacle, and drydock. Many of these shapes are formed when the iceberg begins to melt.

TABULAR

BLOCKY

WEDGE

DOME

PINNACLE

DRYDOCK

The record for the tallest iceberg goes to the Melville Bay Iceberg, sighted off the coast of Greenland in 1958. The iceberg extended out of the water 550 feet (165m), making it almost as tall as the Washington Monument.

A floating iceberg will last between 1 and 3 years after breaking off from its glacier.

The largest iceberg ever sighted came from Greenland and was named the Great Tabular. This enormous flat shelf of ice was roughly the size of the state of Rhode Island.

By studying the crystal structure of an iceberg, geologists can determine which glacier it came from.

One the most enormous lava flows in the world is in central Oregon in the United States. About 1,300 years ago, a volcano spewed more than 170 million cubic yards (130 million cubic meters) of molten rock. This is enough to pave 70,000 miles (13,000 km) of road—a road that could circle Earth three times.

From 50 to 70 volcanoes erupt each year, and about 160 erupt each decade.

Historically, Indonesia has experienced more volcanic eruptions than any other country. During the past 10,000 years, geologists estimate that 76 active volcanoes have erupted about 1,171 times.

Most volcanic eruptions last a single day. However, the volcanoes Etna and Stomboli in Italy, Erte Ale in Ethiopia, Manam in New Guinea, and Sakurajima in Japan have been erupting continually during the past three decades.

The world's tallest volcano is Ojos del Salado, which straddles the countries of Chile and Argentina. The cone rises 22,595 feet (6,779m). The next nine tallest volcanoes are all in the same region.

At any given moment during the day or night, at least 20 volcanoes are erupting throughout the world.

The dust from the 1980 explosion of Mount St. Helens was so extensive that it covered half the state of Washington.

THE BIGGEST ISLANDS

* Greenland, with 839,999 square miles (2,175,596 square km), is the largest island;

* New Guinea (316,615 square miles or 820,032 square km) is the second largest;

* Borneo (286,914 square miles or 743,106 square km) is the third;

* Madagascar (226,657 square miles or 587,041 square km) is the fourth;

* Baffin (183,810 square miles or 476,067 square km) is the fifth;

* Sumatra (182,859 square miles or 473,604 square km) is the sixth;

* Honshu (88,925 square miles or 230,315 square km) is the seventh;

* Great Britain (88,758 square miles or 229,883 square km) is the eighth.

Caves often have as many as three ecosystems: the warm, dry climate surrounding the entrance; the warm, moist microclimate at the entrance; and the cool, moist, dark environment of the cave itself.

The term *speleothem* refers to the various types of mineral deposit formations found in caves, such as stalactites, stalagmites, columns, flowstone formations, and draperies.

Speleothem are formed when mineral-rich groundwater flows through cracks in cave walls or ceilings. As the water evaporates, the minerals accumulate into fantastic shapes.

Mammoth Cave in central Kentucky is the longest cave system in the world. The system, 10 miles (16km) in diameter, consists of 345 miles (555km) of irregular passageways, underground lakes, and rivers.

A stalactite is an icicle-shaped formation that hangs down from the ceiling of a cave. The Antiparos Cave on the Greek island of the same name has some of the world's most spectacular stalactites—many over 20 feet (6m) long.

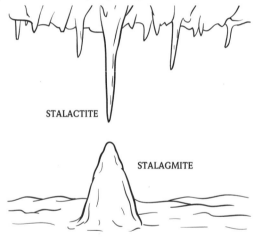

STALACTITE

STALAGMITE

A stalagmite is a cone-shaped formation that grows upward from the floor of a cave. They're usually wider, lower, and fatter than stalactites.

Draperies, one of the most beautiful formations in caves, are the result of groundwater running in a sheet down an inclined ceiling. The resulting translucent sheet of striped color often resembles a strip of bacon.

The most unusual feature of the Waitomo Cave system of North Island, New Zealand, is the thousands of glowworms that attach themselves to the cave ceiling. Visitors can walk through the dark chambers and see a spectacular "starry sky."

Groundwater in caves, flowing in a film over dirt and rock, can form a bumpy calcite layer that looks like a waterfall. Geologists call this a flowstone formation.

The world's largest natural underground space is part of the Mulu cave system in Indonesia. Called the Sarawak Chamber, it's 2,300 feet (690m) long, 1,480 feet (444m) wide, and 230 feet (69m) high—large enough to contain 40 Boeing 747 jets or 7,500 buses.

Wyandotte Cave in southern Indiana contains the largest underground mountain—135 feet (40.5m) high!

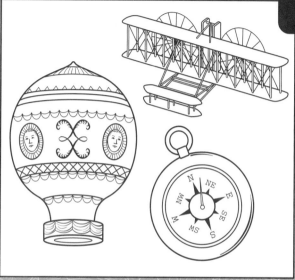

9

Good ideas have a way of rising to the top, and the following chapter lists some of the best ideas of all time. Think about it—for 8,000 years, people all over the globe have been thinking and tinkering. Where would we be without their efforts?

IDEAS AND INVENTIONS

The abacus was invented in Mesopotamia, probably by the Babylonians. Over the next 2,000 years, it made its way to Europe and East Asia.

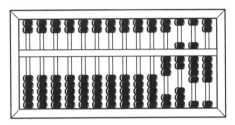

Neither the ancient Greeks nor the early Christians used the numeral zero. The concept of zero came from India, and reached Europe through the Arab world.

The first recipe for gunpowder comes from the Song Dynasty of China, around A.D. 1044. The Chinese were probably using it long before this, however, for fireworks.

The first treatise on perspective was written in 480 B.C. by the Greek artist Agatharkhos, a scene painter for the theatre.

The potter's wheel is among the earliest of inventions, appearing simultaneously in China, Sumeria, and Egypt around 4000 B.C. Some archeologists speculate that it was used long before the concept of the wheel was applied to vehicles.

The first evidence of the use of a mechanical drill is in a marble pedestal in the Domus Aurea or "Golden House" of the Roman emperor Nero, made in about A.D. 74.

The pocket watch was invented in around 1500 by the German clock maker Peter Henlein. Both "Henlein's Morsel" and its inventor were ridiculed at the time.

The oldest mechanical clock is located in England's Salisbury Cathedral. Dating from the 13th century, the clock features a system of gears and ropes that would ring the tower bells every hour. Although the clock is no longer kept wound, it was demonstrated recently and found to work perfectly.

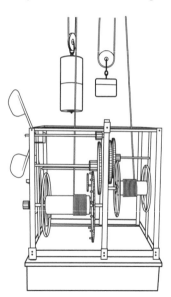

Optical fiber, those light-carrying threads that are used in communication (and to decorate Christmas trees) was invented in 1966 by the British inventors Charles Kao and George Hockham.

Paper was invented in China in about 100 B.C. But the physician Ts'ai Lun greatly improved it in A.D. 105 by adding tree bark and soft woods. This ancient paper was of very high quality and came to be known as "Marquis Ts'ai Paper."

The Chinese were the first to design gunfire-powered cannons. They used them to defend themselves against the Mongol threat from the north.

We owe our 60-based time system (60 minutes to the hour; 60 seconds to the minute) to the Babylonians.

The crossbow was invented in China in around 500 B.C. and was made from highly tempered bronze. The invention reached Europe about 400 years later.

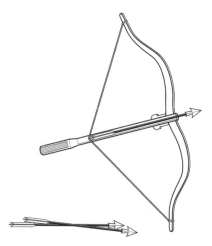

The first scuba diving gear was invented in 1771 by the British engineer John Smeaton. The diver wore a barrel that was connected to a boat on the surface by a hose. Air was pumped through the hose by the diver's companion.

One hour before Alexander Graham Bell registered his patent for the telephone in 1876, Elisha Grey patented his design. After years of lawsuits between the two inventors, the patent went to Bell.

For more than 15 years after its invention, the telephone wasn't widely appreciated because people thought it was practically useless.

In 1876, a memo that circulated among top executives at Western Union stated: "The telephone has too many shortcomings to be seriously considered as a means of communication."

Alexander Graham Bell advised Mark Twain to invest $5,000 in the telephone. Twain declined, saying he didn't think telephones had "much of a practical future."

In 1910, the British Parliament stated that there was no need for telephones in the Parliament chambers because "we have enough messengers here."

The Monopoly game was invented by Charles Darrow in 1933. He sold the rights to George Parker in 1935.

The American board game entrepreneur George Parker invented more than 100 games, including Pit, Rook, Flinch, Risk, and Clue.

The hair perm was invented in 1906 by Karl Ludwig Nessler of Germany.

The very first projection of an image on a screen was made by a German priest. In 1646, Athanasius Kircher used a candle or oil lamp to project hand-painted images onto a white screen.

In 1894, Thomas Edison and W.K.L. Dickson introduced the first film camera.

The arch was the most important structural invention of ancient Roman architecture because it allowed engineers to build higher. Sometimes "blind" arches, or arches without openings, were built into high walls to help distribute the weight of the bricks evenly.

An earthquake-detecting machine, or *seismograph*, was invented in China in about A.D. 200. The design consisted of small stone balls delicately balanced on fulcrums. The slightest tremor would cause the balls to drop onto a sounding drum. Its creator was the philosopher Chang Heng, who became wealthy from his invention.

The Chinese were the first to invent movable type, in about A.D. 1040. The inventor was Bi Sheng.

The first vending machine was created in about 215 B.C. by the Greek inventor Hero of Alexandria. When a coin was dropped into a slot, the weight of the coin would trip a lever that allowed a measured quantity of water to spill out.

The earliest Roman calendar was based on the motion of the moon and contained 355 days. The first month was Martius, which later became March in the Julian calendar. The following lunar months were Aprilis, Maius, Junius, Quinctilis, Sextilis, September, October, November, December, Januarius, and Februarius.

During the 1860s, the French inventor George LeClanche developed the dry-cell battery, the basis for modern batteries.

The Chinese first started weaving silk (or *si* in Chinese) about 5,000 years ago.

HYPATIA'S DEVICES

The first device for distilling water was invented in ancient Egypt by a woman named Hypatia of Alexandria. She was the daughter of Theon, a mathematician who taught at the great school at the Alexandrine Library. Hypatia also invented several measuring devices, including hygrometers (for measuring humidity), astrolabes, and planispheres.

In about 500 B.C., the Greek philosopher Herakleitos introduced what modern physicists call the flux theory. This means that the universe is never the same from moment to moment. Herakleitos was fond of telling his students, "It is not possible to step into the same river twice."

In 1893, a Missouri doctor created peanut butter as a food for invalids. By 1895, J.H. Kellogg of the cereal family was making peanut butter at his health spa and recommending it for patients with bad teeth.

The first human passengers in a hot air balloon were the physicist Pilatre de Rozier and the officer Francois D'Arlandes. They took their ride in 1785, cruising for about 28 minutes over the city of Paris at a height of 3,300 feet (1,006m).

The first hot air balloon passengers were anima[l]s: a sheep, a duck, and a goat. They lifted off f[rom] Versailles in September of 1783 and were watch[ed] by Louis XVI and Marie Antoinette. The flig[ht] lasted 8 minutes, and the balloon traveled 2.17 miles (3.5km), reaching a height of 1,650 feet (503m) before descending.

fter the French Revolution of 1789, the revolutionaries tried to introduce a form of "decimal time," consisting of two cycles of 10-hour days. The people hated it and refused to follow it.

Early mechanical clocks used wooden gears instead of metal ones. Metal gears required lubrication, and since animal oil was used at the time, the gears would stick and require frequent cleaning.

The compass was invented by the Chinese around A.D. 100. They called it *zhi nan zhen*, which means "south-pointing needle." The Europeans didn't have compasses until about 1400.

Flax, cultivated about 12,000 years ago in Syria and Anatolia (now Turkey), is the earliest known plant source for fiber. It is also an important source of oil.

Sausage is one of the oldest forms of processed food. It was even mentioned in Homer's *Odyssey* in the 9th century B.C.

In the 1920s, the future president of RCA, David Sarnoff, tried to convince his friends in the wireless industry that radio was a great investment opportunity. After a meeting, he was sent a memo that stated, "The wireless music box has no imaginable commercial value. Who would pay for a message sent to nobody in particular?"

The discovery of vitamins took place in 1912. An American chemist, Frederick Hopkins, found chemical compounds in foods that he felt were essential to human health. He isolated them and extracted them. His colleague, Casimir Funk, named these compounds "vitamines."

The first person to isolate vitamin C was the Czech scientist Albert Szent-Gyögyi, who extracted it from paprika. In 1937 he received the Nobel Prize for his accomplishment.

Cellophane tape was invented in 1930 by Richard Drew, an engineer working at the 3M Company.

The paperclip was invented and patented in 1899 by the Connecticut inventor William Middlebrook.

In 1945, the Volkswagen company, along with all its factories and patents, was offered to Henry Ford II—for free. He turned it down because he thought the Volkswagen "Beetle" was a bad design.

In 1823, the Irish scientist Dionysius Lardner didn't believe high-speed trains were possible. He wrote that passengers on such a train would die of suffocation.

The Wright Brothers were not the first to success-fully fly a plane. A year before their famous flight in 1903, a New Zealand farmer named Richard Pearse built and successfully tested his own machine. And a year before that, Gustave Whitehead flew a machine about a half mile over a field in Connecticut.

Ferdinand Graf von Zeppelin, a German military officer, developed the first rigid dirigible, a lighter-than-air craft, in 1900.

The word "sneaker" comes from Henry McKinney, an advertising executive. He liked the way the quiet rubber sole of the shoe allowed its wearers to "sneak" around.

Wheat and barley were cultivated more than 10,000 years ago. Scientist know this by examining the grain particles found on ancient flint sickles and grinding stones.

Traffic lights were used before cars appeared on the streets. The lights were used to route pedestrians and horse-drawn carriages.

Although Napoleon was "canning" food for his army in wine bottles as early as 1809, the process of antiseptic canning wasn't patented until 1825.

The rotary can opener was invented 48 years after cans were introduced.

In 200 B.C., the mathematician Eratosthenes accurately computed the circumference of Earth.

Count Alessandro Volta invented the first battery, consisting of copper disks and brine, in the 18th century.

In 1604 the Italian astronomer Galileo designed a pendulum clock, but never built one.

The artificial grass we know as AstroTurf was invented in 1965 by Monsanto scientists James Faria and Robert Wright. It was first used to carpet a school in Rhode Island. Later that year, it was chosen for covering the field in the Houston Astrodome.

The first fax system, invented in 1842 by the Scottish clockmaker Alexander Bain, consisted of swinging a pendulum over metallic type. Contact with the type caused an electric current to flow over wires to a distant swinging pendulum synchronized with the first. Chemically treated paper was placed under the second pendulum and produced a brown image when the current passed from the pendulum to the paper.

It took 6 minutes to send a single-page by fax in 1924. In 1974, it took 3 minutes, and by 1980, 1 minute. Today, a single-page fax takes about 2 seconds.

Magnavox manufactured and Xerox marketed the first commercial fax machine in 1966.

A fax machine cost about $20,000 in 1982.

During battles, the ancient Chinese used specially designed "warrior kites" to drop flaming pitch over enemy lines.

The first photograph to be transmitted via fax was sent in 1904 by American inventor Arthur Korn.

The Italian explorer Marco Polo brought porcelain to Europe in the 14th century.

A fine clay called kaolin was utilized to make porcelain in China around A.D. 1280. A cruder form of porcelain, called seladon, had been developed 200 years earlier.

In ancient Rome, wooden cranes were often used to hoist heavy materials. From wall paintings that survive, modern engineers can see details of their construction, and that some cranes were powered by as many as 50 men walking on large treadmills.

Although Leonardo da Vinci sketched a bicycle design in one of his notebooks, the Frenchman Edouard De Sivrac built the first bicycle-type vehicle in 1690.

The modern bicycle looks almost exactly the same as a bicycle from around 1900.

The first submarine was designed in 1578 by an English mathematician. The first submarine was built in 1620 by Cornelius van Drebbel, a Dutch inventor.

In 1776, the American colonist David Bushnell built the first submarine used for military purposes. Used in the American Revolution, his one-man "Turtle" was powered by hand-cranked wooden propellers.

Air-filled tires were used on bicycles before they were used on cars.

The first machine to show animated movies was called the "wheel of life" and patented by William Lincoln in 1867. The machine, lit by an arc lamp, showed a series of drawings, which appeared to move when rotated and then viewed through a slit.

THE FIRST PLYWOOD?

A 4,700-year-old coffin from an Egyptian pyramid at Saqqara was found to be made of six layers of wood veneer, sandwiched and glued together like plywood. The woods were cypress, juniper, and cedar of Lebanon.

Around 1750, the first glue formula was patented in Britain. It used fish oil.

The ancient Greek natural philosopher Anaxagoras (500-428 B.C.) taught that the sun and stars were made of red-hot stone, ignited by friction as they circled the Earth. His theories might have been influenced by a meteorite that fell near his home in 467 B.C.

A type of aerosol spray can was first introduced in France around 1790. The can contained a pressurized carbonated beverage.

OCKHAM'S RAZOR

In the year 1324, the English philosopher William of Ockham wrote that the simplest explanation is usually the most accurate—or "What can be accounted for by fewer assumptions is explained in vain by more." This approach came to be known as "Ockham's Razor," and proved valuable in scientific research.

In 1455, Gutenburg printed the first bible with movable type. Soon after this, he published books on herbs, medicines, and "simples" (herbs combined into teas and powders)—all of which became best sellers.

In 1824, the English scientist Michael Faraday invented the rubber balloon to use in his experiments with hydrogen gas.

In the early 20th century, the British mathematician Lord Kelvin predicted that radio had no future. He also predicted that heavier-than-air flying machines were impossible.

In 1912, Marechal Foch, the Professor of Strategy at the École Supérieure de Guerre in France, proclaimed: "Airplanes are interesting toys but of no military value."

Human speech was first transmitted over the ocean by radio in 1915. The broadcast began in New York City and was heard at the Eiffel Tower in Paris.

In 1899, the director of the U.S. Patent Office assured President McKinley that "everything that can be invented has already been invented."

THE FIRST WEATHERMAN

Greek philosopher Euktemon (50 B.C.) might be considered the first meteorologist. Along with designing calendars, Euktemon identified and predicted weather patterns and announced his weekly forecasts in the marketplace.

Albert Einstein applied for and was granted a patent for an improved butane-ammonia refrigerator in 1927.

The Greek poet and philosopher Xenophanes (580-460 B.C.) was the first to write a treatise on fossils. From his studies of fossilized fish, he concluded that all land was once beneath the sea and would eventually return there.

In 1973, the first airbag was introduced by Chevrolet as an optional feature.

George Westinghouse, the founder of Westinghouse Electric, invented air brakes in 1868.

The Greek physician Hippocrates wrote numerous works on medicinal plants. When he was condemned to death by the Greek senate, he took his own life by drinking hemlock—the juice of which he had identified as poisonous in one of his own volumes.

Aluminum foil was first commercially produced in 1910 by a Swiss company. Before that, metal foil was made from pounded tin.

Actor Zeppo Marx of the Marx Brothers applied for and received a patent for a "cardiac pulse rate monitor" in 1969.

WHAT IS A SECOND?

Today, timekeeping has moved away from the mechanical and is based on the motions of atomic particles. For example, the interval of one second is now defined by the way the atoms behave in the element cesium. The motion of a cesium atom regularly changes from a quiet to an excited state, and physicists call this a "transition." A second equals 9,192,631,770 transitions of the cesium atom and is extremely precise.

Before 1840, paper manufacturers used rags instead of wood pulp.

The idea of an ambulance probably started in the 11th century with the Knights of St. John. This was a group of people who would assist soldiers injured on the battlefields during the Crusades.

In 1872, the professor of physiology at Toulouse University called Louis Pasteur's theory of germs a "ridiculous fiction."

The first Crayola crayon was black and made of charcoal mixed with oil.

The first color Crayola crayon was produced in 1903 by the inventors Edwin Binney and Harold Smith.

The name "Crayola" was suggested by the inventor's wife. Alice Binney combined the French word for chalk, *craie*, with *ola* for oily.

Over 100 billion Crayola crayons have been produced since their invention, there were originally eight colors in a box. In 1998 the biggest box contained 120.

Thomas Edison filed 1,093 patents in his lifetime, including 34 patents for the telephone, 141 for batteries, 150 for the telegraph, and 389 for electric light and power.

In 1770, the English chemist Joseph Priestley coined the name "rubber" for the natural latex of the South American *Hevia brasiliensis* tree. Priestley noted that latex was excellent for rubbing out the marks of a black pencil on paper.

In 1944, Chinese botanists discovered a living specimen of the dawn redwood tree. Before this discovery, the tree was known only through 20-million-year-old fossil samples and thought to be extinct.

Samuel Clemens (Mark Twain) patented a design for a self-pasting scrapbook in 1873.

A device for tying ships to keep them stable while freight was unloaded was patented by President Abraham Lincoln in 1849.

The candy cane was created in 1670, when the choirmaster at the Cologne Cathedral in Germany bent sugar sticks to represent a shepherd's staff. He gave the white canes to children to keep them quiet during the long Christmas services. It wasn't until 1900 that striped candy canes began to be sold in America.

Bubble gum was created in 1906 by American inventor Frank Fleer. He called it "Blibber-Blubber Gum." The recipe was perfected in 1928 by Walter Diemer, who colored the gum pink and called it "Double Bubble."

The inventor of cotton candy was Thomas Patton. He received a patent for a cotton candy machine in 1900, and the first cotton candy was sold at the Ringling Bros. Circus the same year.

The doughnut was invented by the American Captain Hanson Crockett Gregory in 1847. He wanted to improve his mother's fried cakes, which were always undercooked and doughy in the middle. His solution? Remove the middle so that the dough could fry evenly.

Gelatin as a dessert was first introduced in 1845 by millionaire industrialist and inventor Peter Cooper. But the product wasn't popular with consumers and Cooper sold his patent. By 1906, the sales of fruit-flavored "Jell-O" reached $1 million.

The candy "Life Savers" was invented in 1912 by chocolate manufacturer Clarence Crane of Cleveland, Ohio. He promoted them as a "summer candy" that wouldn't melt in the heat like chocolate. The original mints looked like life preservers, hence the name.

The lollipop was invented in 1916 by Samuel Born, a Russian immigrant who invented a machine that inserted a stick into a molten sugar disk. Born also invented those chocolate sprinkles we love to put on ice cream.

In 1905, eleven-year-old Frank Epperson left his fruit drink with a stirrer outside overnight. The result was a frozen popsicle, originally called the "Epsicle."

The potato chip was invented in 1853 by George Crum, a cook at the Moon Lake Lodge in Saratoga Springs, New York. A fussy customer returned fried potatoes that were too thick, and Crum, a temperamental cook, sliced the potatoes so thin that they couldn't be eaten with a fork. The customer loved them, and a new treat was born.

The game of chess was invented in China about 2,200 years ago, before moving on to Persia (now Iran). Pieces were carved in the form of elephants, horses, foot soldiers, and chariots.

The game of checkers or draughts goes back about 5,000 years. A version of it very similar to the modern ones was found in the ruins of the ancient city of Ur in present-day Iraq.

The crossword puzzle was created by journalist Arthur Wynne. On Sunday December 21, 1913, a diamond-shaped puzzle appeared in the newspaper *The New York World*.

The jigsaw puzzle was invented in 1767 by the English teacher John Spilsbury. To teach geography to his students, he glued maps to hardwood boards and then sawed up the boards into the shapes of the individual countries.

The most popular puzzle in history, the Rubix Cube, was invented in 1974 by Hungarian mathematician Erno Rubik. There's only one correct way to assemble the cube and 43 quintillion (43 followed by eighteen zeros) wrong ways!

The first remote control for a television was invented in 1950 by the Zenith Corporation of America. Called the "Lazy Bone," it was attached to the television by a thick wire. Five years later, Zenith created the first wireless remote, the "Flash-matic."

The first ferris wheel was built for the 1893 Chicago World's Fair. Its inventor was George W. Ferris, a bridge builder.

The trampoline was invented in 1936 by George Nissen, an American circus acrobat and Olympic medalist. He called it a "flashfold."

The roller coaster was invented in Ohio by a toboggan designer, John Miller. In 1926, Miller patented his "Flying Turns" ride, which featured cars sliding down inclined ramps. It would be several years later before Miller added tracks to his design.

Nonshrinking cotton fabric was created in 1930 by the inventor Sanford Cluett of the Sanforizer Company. Cluett created an ammonia-based bath process that caused cotton fibers to swell, preventing shrinkage when washed.

In 1994, the first genetically engineered vegetable, the "Flavr-Savr Tomato," was approved for commercial marketing. The tomato was designed for slow ripening and increased shelf life.

The Chinese invented the umbrella over 4,000 years ago by waxing their paper parasols, used for sun protection, to keep dry in the rain.

The ancient Romans were the first to understand and practice crop rotation—the alternate planting of legumes and grains. The legumes replaced the nitrogen in the soil and ensured a more plentiful grain harvest.

The Ancient Romans invented the hourglass around A.D. 100, supposedly to time the orations of speakers in the Roman Senate.

10

In case you haven't noticed, computers—with all their advantages and complications—are here to stay. Some say they're the greatest invention since the wheel; others claim they've only confused and complicated our lives. Here's a collection of people, events, terms, and definitions from the computer world. You be the judge!

COMPUTER CRAZINESS

297

Before computers were in use, navigators, astronomers, accountants, and mathematicians all relied on books of tables—most of which were filled with mistakes.

The first version of Microsoft Windows was released on November 20, 1985. It sold for $99.

The "8-Second Rule" means that someone will wait no more than 8 seconds for a web page to load before moving on to another web page. This rule of thumb is used by webmasters to keep their pages uncomplicated.

The expression "whack a mole" means closing an annoying pop-up window while Internet surfing.

An angry e-mail, newsgroup, or chatroom message that attacks another writer is called a "flame."

Those happy, sad, or angry faces that sometimes accompany messages sent in chatrooms or posted on message boards are called "emoticons." The word combines "emotion" with "icon."

In the book *2001: A Space Odyssey*, the supercomputer HAL was built in 1997.

The acronym TWAIN, an interface that's used to scan images, stands for "Technology Without An Interesting Name."

More software has been written for PCs than for any other system on the market.

The word *modem*, the device that allows your computer to communicate with other computers, is a combination of the words "modulator" and "demodulator."

Digital modems were developed in the 1950s by the U.S. Department of Defense and designed to transmit data over the public phone system from computer to computer. Because analog circuits could only recognize signals within the frequency range of the human voice, the modem was designed to transmit outside those frequency limitations.

The first commercially available modem was manufactured in 1962 and had a speed of 300 bits (or bauds, in modem terminology) per second.

The processing speed of a computer's chip is measured in megahertz (MHz). The higher the megahertz rate of the chip, the faster your computer calculates. Megahertz rate is also called the "clock speed" of the computer.

The clock speed of the original IBM personal computer was 4.77 megahertz. Today's computers are nearly 500 times faster.

A standard compact disc (CD) is 4.8 inches (12cm) in diameter.

You can store 74 minutes of music on a CD, equivalent to 783,216,000 bytes of information.

On a CD, information is "written" from the inside center hole to the outside edge.

Unlike a data tape, a CD has only one track, which spirals from the CD's center hole to its edge. Since the data is stored in a spiral, a greater concentration of it exists at the center of the CD than towards its edge.

If all the data on a CD were stretched out in a single line, it would be 3.5 miles (5.6km) long.

The first graphical computer game, "Tic-Tac-Toe," was created in 1952 by A.S. Douglas at the University of Cambridge. The game displayed crude symbols on a cathode ray tube attached to the computer's processor.

The first animated video game was created in 1958 by William Higinbotham at the Brookhaven National Laboratory in New York. It was called "Tennis for Two."

The first game designed exclusively for a computer monitor was called "SpaceWar." It was created in 1962 by the programmer Steve Russell.

In 1972, the first home video game console was released by the Magnavox Corporation. Called "Odyssey," it came programmed with 12 games and was designed by Ralph Baer.

THE WORLD'S FIRST MICROCOMPUTER

In January 1975, the magazine *Popular Electronics* featured a picture of the Altair 8800 computer—the world's first small, self-contained computer—built by a company in New Mexico. It was sold by mail order, came with a build-it-yourself kit, including a front panel with a grid of lights (no monitor), and 256 bytes of memory. It cost $397.

The first person to use the word "virus" to describe a destructive piece of computer code was Fred Cohen, a student at the University of Southern California, in 1983. He used the word in his Ph.D. dissertation.

In 1988, one of the most destructive viruses was unleashed on the world. Called "Jerusalem," it activated itself every Friday the 13th for nearly eight years before being destroyed by virus-detecting software.

THE TROJAN HORSE VIRUS

Initially a hoax (before someone finally created a real one called AOL4FREE), a Trojan Horse virus generally appears as an e-mail with a funny attachment. The attachment might look like a joke, a screen saver, a picture, or even a note from a friend. But it is actually a miniature program of executable files. Once you open it, it will install itself in your computer and run—"infecting" programs and personal data, or sending confidential information like passwords to other computers. Unlike other viruses, however, a Trojan Horse does not reproduce itself.

There are true viruses and virus hoaxes. A true virus is a small program attached to an e-mail message. When the program is opened, it attacks the computer's system. A hoax is an e-mail with no attachment, but it warns users about a new virus and instructs them to "protect" themselves by making destructive changes on their computer.

In 1990, the Symantec Corporation released antivirus software, one of the first programs of its kind in the world.

A worm virus doesn't infect other programs but reproduces itself and spreads, mostly by e-mail. Like a true living organism, a worm wants to reproduce and survive. By attaching itself to your e-mail software and sending copies of itself to everyone in your address book, the worm keeps itself going.

THE BABBAGE DIFFERENCE ENGINE

The most amazing mechanical calculator ever thought up, although never completed, was the Babbage Difference Engine. Frustrated by the many mistakes he found while examining calculations for the Royal Astronomical Society, Charles Babbage (1791–1871) decided to create a giant calculator—powered by steam. Before the British government stopped funding the project in 1842, the Difference Engine had over 500,000 pieces, took programming instructions from perforated cards, and had a memory chamber for 1,000 numerals up to 50 digits long. Babbage is considered the father of computing technology.

A "denial of service" (DoS) attack involves sending huge amounts of useless data, or spam, to servers, overwhelming them so that they become paralyzed.

On October 23, 2002, a denial of service attack targeted 9 important international servers, paralyzing them for about 2 hours. These giant servers stored thousands of domain addresses such as AOL's.

COLAMAR'S ARITHOMETER

In 1829, the Frenchman Charles Xavier Thomas de Colamar invented a dial and lever machine that could perform the four basic arithmetic functions—addition, subtraction, multiplication, and division. This mechanical calculator came into widespread use, and the device was popular up until World War I.

The bar code was patented in 1952 by Joseph Woodland and Bernard Silver. In June of 1974, the first bar code scanner was installed at a Marsh's supermarket in Troy, Ohio. The first product to carry a bar code was Wrigley's gum.

THE FIRST PERSONAL COMPUTER

IBM introduced the personal computer, or PC, in 1981. This was the first machine made for people to use in their homes or offices. As copies, or clones, of the PC flooded the marketplace, computer use jumped from 2 million in 1981 to 5.5 million in 1982. By 2002, 120 million PCs were being used.

Before 1981, there were two competing computer designs—Apple and IBM. With the success of IBM's first personal computer in 1981, the balance shifted away from Apple, as millions of PC clones flooded the marketplace.

Apple Computer began in Steve Jobs' Cupertino, California, garage.

The apple logo on Apple Computer was the idea of Steve Jobs, the founder of the company, who was eating an apple when assembling his first computer. He enhanced his apple logo with a conspicuous bitemark. The mark was supposed to indicate a "byte."

The Apple I computer was unveiled in April 1976 at the Homebrew Computer Club in Palo Alto, California. It was sold through several small retailers, but those wishing to buy one (at a cost of $666.66) received only the circuit board. They had to build the case themselves.

Only 220 copies of the 1976 Apple I computer were produced. It's considered to be the most prized computer collectable today, worth about $60,000 and increasing in value every year.

John Sculley, a former executive of Apple, was enticed away from PepsiCo by Apple founder Steve Jobs, who convinced Sculley to join Apple by asking: "Do you want to contribute to something important or spend the rest of your life making sugar water?"

There are exactly 8,589,934,592 bits in a gigabyte.

In the 1970s, the term microcomputer was used to describe a computer that had its own independent processing power and was not connected to a main-frame, or master computer.

THE BIRTH OF IBM

The American inventor Herman Hollerith wanted to design a machine that provided a faster way to compute the United States Census. The need for such a machine was important, since the government worried that, with the population increase, counting all U.S. citizens would take over 10 years. Hollerith applied the mechanics of a loom to his punch card design machine, which provided accurate computations and stored data efficiently. The business world soon expressed interest in his machine, and in 1896, Hollerith founded the Tabulating Machine Company—later to become IBM.

In 1982, *Time* magazine's "Person of the Year" cover was entitled "Machine of the Year" and featured a computer.

A Chatterbot is a program that runs in a chatroom and simulates a chatting human.

The first electronic mail, or "e-mail," was sent in 1972 by Ray Tomlinson. It was sent between two computers that were actually sitting beside each other. The first e-mail message was "QWERTYUIOP" (the letters in the top row of the typewriter keyboard).

It was computer engineer Ray Tomlinson's idea to use the @ sign to separate the name of the user from the name of the computer in an e-mail address.

The initials URL stand for "Universal Resource Locator," a fancy term for an Internet address such as http://www.google.com.

If an Internet address (URL) ends with an ".org" it means that the organization is not commercial, but either nonprofit or private.

Bell Labs first came up with the idea of a cellular phone in 1948.

The compact disk was invented in 1965 by James Russell. But the disk came into popularity only when it was mass-produced by the Philips Company in 1980.

The BASIC computer language was invented in 1963 at Dartmouth College in New Hampshire by mathematicians John Kemeny and Tom Kurtzas. BASIC stands for "Beginner's All-Purpose Symbolic Instruction Code."

According to the magazine *Scientific American*, the next generation of protein-based computers will be 1,000 times faster than today's silicon-based computers.

Although several radio stations in the U.S. have managed to acquire domain names ending with .FM, the suffix really belongs to the Federated States of Micronesia.

The inkjet printer was invented in 1976, but didn't become popular until Hewlett-Packard released an "affordable" model of it—at $1,000—in 1988.

Most computer keyboards are extremely touch-sensitive. Holding down a function key for more than a half second can cause that key to repeat its instructions eight times per second.

The first IBM personal computer used a 5.25–inch (13-cm) floppy disk to store its operating system and programs. A year later, IBM introduced a new feature—a "fixed disk" with 10 megabytes of memory. Later the name was changed to "hard drive."

THE BIGGEST CALCULATOR

During World War II, governments recognized the importance of computers in military strategy. In 1944, Harvard engineer Howard Aiken succeeded in producing the first all-electronic calculator for creating ballistic charts for the U.S. Navy. His machine was half the length of a football field and contained more than 500 miles (850km) of wiring.

IBM called its first laptop computer "The Convertible." It was the size of a suitcase.

ENIAC—THE WARTIME ELECTRONIC BRAIN

The most famous and powerful computer to come out of World War II was the Electronic Numerical Integrator and Computer (ENIAC), funded by the U.S. government and designed by the University of Pennsylvania. ENIAC had 18,000 vacuum tubes, 70,000 resistors, and 5 million soldered joints. The computer was so massive that it consumed 160 kilowatts of power—enough energy to dim the lights in an entire section of Philadelphia!

The design of the computer keyboard evolved from the typewriter keyboard, which was invented in 1868.

In computer terminology, "protocol" means a set of rules for exchanging data that both sides, in this case two computers, agree to follow.

BIRTH OF THE CHIP

Although transistors were responsible for smaller, more efficient computers, they were also hot and could damage a computer's wiring system. To get around this problem, engineers began looking at the electrical conducting properties of silicon, made from quartz. In 1958, Jack Kilby, an engineer with Texas Instruments, developed the 3-component integrated circuit or "chip." This made much smaller computers possible. The chip was ahead of its time, and unfortunately, Kilby didn't renew his patent by the time chips became a standard feature in every computer.

In July of 1993, a fire destroyed Japan's Sumitomo Chemical Company. Since Sumitomo supplied over 60% of the world's cresol (used to make memory chips), the price of memory chips skyrocketed.

THE FIRST COMPUTER TO SUCCESSFULLY PREDICT A PRESIDENTIAL ELECTION

In the mid-1940s, engineer John von Neumann made important improvements in computer design. His "stored memory" design allowed a computer to handle more-complicated programs, and his idea for a central processing unit (CPU) allowed electronic functions to be concentrated in a single source. In 1951, the UNIVAC I (Universal Automatic Computer) became the first computer to use these features. One of UNIVAC's impressive early achievements was predicting that Dwight D. Eisenhower would win the 1952 presidential election.

The language used to create web pages is called HTML, which stands for "hypertext markup language." HTML allows webmasters to insert special tags into their pages that tell the browser how to display text and graphics.

Computers that store and deliver information to other computers across the Internet are called *servers*. They "serve" by receiving a request from your PC, called a client, and delivering the data.

A fumbling beginner on the Internet is sometimes referred to as a "newbie."

The standard protocol for sending e-mail is SMTP, for "simple mail transfer protocol." This protocol packages your message into a kind of envelope and sends it to a series of servers. Each server leaves information on the message so that the receiver may see the message route.

The term RGB stands for red, green, and blue. It was a standard for color television tubes, and was later adapted for computer monitor screens.

The initials TCP/IP stand for Transmission Control Protocol/Internet Protocol, a set of rules that allows computers to exchange data across the Internet. The Department of Defense developed TCP/IP and it has since been widely adopted as a networking standard.

A portal is a kind of "lobby" that an Internet user will visit before going on the Web. Many portals started out as search engines.

Before portals like Yahoo or MSN, text-based Bulletin Board Services (BBSs) were popular online meeting places for people with modems. One of the first ones was America Online (AOL).

Of the millions of colors a computer can produce, only 216 of them look identical on both an Apple computer and a PC. Web developers use these "browser safe colors" to make sure that their pages look the same for owners of either machine.

The first computer game designed to be played on a television set was created in 1967. Its inventor, Ralph Baer, got the idea while working in television.

A game called "Computer Space" was the first arcade game, created in 1971 by programmer Nolan Bushnell. It was followed by another popular game, "Pong." A year later, Bushnell and Ted Dabney started the Atari computer company.

The company SUN Microsystems took its name from the Stanford University Network.

The computer "mouse" got its name from its inventor, Douglas Engelbart of Stanford University. He called it a mouse because the "tail came out of the end," and patented his invention in 1970.

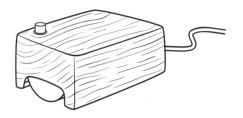

According to *Wired* magazine, one of the computer industry's standard-setters, the plural of "mouse" is "mouses."

The Silicon Graphics computer—one of the most expensive machines ever produced—was used to create the special effects for the movies *Forrest Gump* and *The Matrix*.

Current Internet IP addresses are 32-bits long. The next generation of addresses, IPv6, will be 128-bits long.

The first DVD players appeared in Japan in November of 1996. To produce a DVD player, a company has to license more than 70 patents owned by different companies.

A person who subscribes to and reads a Usenet newsgroup but never contributes to it is called a "lurker."

The first "Speak and Spell" software, simulating the human voice, was introduced in 1978.

"Zipping" means converting CD files into a compressed file format for storing or transferring.

In 1970, the engineer James Fergason invented the first liquid crystal display, or LCD. Liquid crystals are display panels—used in devices such as wristwatches—that reflect light when voltage is applied.

The Xerox company introduced the first laser printer, the 9700 model, in 1978. It was the first commercially available laser printer in the world and could output 120 pages per minute.

The initials DOS stand for Disk Operating System. DOS was introduced by IBM and originally fit onto two 700K floppy disks.

The programming language FORTRAN, which stands for FORmula TRANslation, was invented by John Backus at IBM. FORTRAN is considered to be the first high-level, or reader-friendly computer language.

Global Positioning System (GPS) technology was invented by the U.S. Department of Defense at a cost of $12-billion in taxpayer money. The system uses satellites and a computer to coordinate the information from those satellites to calculate navigational positions.

One of the most popular computer games ever invented, "Tetris," was created in Russia in the early 1980s but never patented.

The first "touch screen" computer was developed at the University of Kentucky. Dr. Sam Hurst, who taught there, patented his "Elograph" in 1971.

In 1943, Thomas Watson, the chairman of IBM, predicted a world market for "maybe only five computers."

The man responsible for the mostly beige color of computers is Jerry Manock, who was the product designer for Apple Computers in 1977. The color was introduced in the Apple II, the first mass-market computer, because it fit into the color scheme of late 70s offices and didn't show dust.

The refresh rate of a computer screen can exhaust the eye muscles and make it difficult to focus. This is because the eyes are forced to refocus hundreds of times per minute as the screen redraws itself.

"Firmware" is a kind of fixed software that resides in appliances like microwave ovens, televisions, coffee timers, and DVD viewers. It contains basic instructions that remain in memory after the appliance is turned off.

Digital camera technology developed from the same technology that recorded video images. In 1951, the first video tape recorder (VTR) captured live images from television cameras by converting the images into electrical impulses and saving the information onto magnetic tape.

And then there's the most famous quote of all: "640K ought to be enough for anybody."—*Bill Gates*

INDEX